Tom Byrnes

WRITING BESTSELLING TRUE CRIME AND SUSPENSE

Break into the Exciting and Profitable Field of Book, Screenplay, and Television Crime Writing

PRIMA PUBLISHING

PRIMA PUBLISHING and colophon are registered trademarks of Prima Communications, Inc.

Library of Congress Cataloging-in-Publication Data

Byrnes, Tom.
    Writing bestselling true crime and suspense : break into the exciting and profitable field of book, screenplay, and television crime writing / Tom Byrnes.
        p. cm.
    Includes index.
    ISBN 0-7615-1026-5
        1. Crime writing—Authorship.   2. Detective and mystery stories—Authorship.   3. Crime—research.   4. Nonfiction novel—Technique.
    I. Title.
PN3377.5.C75B97 1997
808.3'872—dc21   97-38391
                                                                                        CIP

97 98 99 00 01 HH 10 9 8 7 6 5 4 3 2 1
Printed in the United States of America

How to Order
Single copies may be ordered from Prima Publishing, P.O. Box 1260BK, Rocklin, CA 95677; telephone (916) 632-4400. Quantity discounts are also available. On your letterhead, include information concerning the intended use of the books and the number of books you wish to purchase.

Visit us online at http://www.primapublishing.com

For Lee, Forever

Contents

Contents

Acknowledgments

Special thanks to Scott Anderson, Edna Buchanan, Lowell Cauffiell, Paul Dinas, Janet Faust-Krusi, Jay Fletcher, Doug Grad, Michaela Hamilton, Michael Jaffe, Jessica Lichenstein, Brian Lane, Paula Munier Lee, Mary Ann Lynch, Harry MacLean, Michelle McCormack, Darcy O'Brien, Jack Olsen, Betty Prashker, Shannon Richardson, Fred Rosen, Ann Rule, Katherine Sands, Charles Spicer, Frank von Zurnick, and Steve White, whose insights, talent, advice, and energy made this book possible.

Introduction

True crime delivers some of the best work that creative nonfiction offers. A well-written piece can take a seemingly ordinary setting filled with normal people—a small industrial city in Wisconsin; a town in the open spaces of Montana—and peel back the layers of society to reveal dark secrets that have been kept for years. It can expose universal truths even as it entertains, and it can leave audiences pondering the randomness of life.

Critical distinctions aside, one of the great virtues of true crime writing is that it is one of the very few genres that has an almost universal appeal when it comes to marketability. Whether packaged as a newspaper or magazine article, a nonfiction book, or an adaptation that winds up as a screenplay for television or film, the bottom line is that true crime sells. It always has and always will. Even in cases where the central premise of a story may not be strong enough to merit its own project, the forensic and investigative details of a crime can serve as the foundation for a fictional work or an original script.

While requiring patience, a sharp eye, and a solid sense of story, the essential skills involved in crafting a salable true crime narrative are easily transferable to other forms of writing as well. Everyone borrows from reality to make their work believable and all writers can benefit from expanding their knowledge of story sources and the elements that separate a likely sale from a dead end. Organized to mirror the step-by-step process of discovering, researching, and writing stories based on actual criminal investigations and court cases, this book will provide you with the knowledge to write true crime, mystery, suspense, or fiction that sells.

Filled with practical tips and insights from successful journalists, bestselling authors, leading editors, and film and television producers, it provides details and advice on every phase of investigative nonfiction writing. But a bestseller or box-office smash filled with complex characters, hidden motives, secret lives, and unspeakable acts of violence does not appear out of thin air. The true crime writer's lot is one of painstaking research, false leads, endless interviews, and round after round of fact checking. Beginning with the criteria for choosing a crime and the ways to research information buried in law enforcement and legal systems, and taking you through the processes of getting reluctant sources to divulge information, structuring a narrative, and pitching a proposal, this book puts everything but a pad and pen in your hands.

The rest is up to you.

Chapter One

WRITING FOR THE AGES

The Enduring Appeal of True Crime

We live in an age dominated by images of violent crime. It appears in headlines, newscasts, popular movies, and prime-time programming, drawing attention even as it repels sensibilities. Crime captivates people by providing a glimpse of the forbidden and the illicit, by striking deep into their sense of curiosity over how close danger lies to the safe boundaries of everyday life. When this fascination with the abnormal is woven into a compelling narrative—an article, book, or screenplay—crime can quickly transform the public into a paying audience. The wisdom of the old adage aside, the simple fact is that crime *does* pay—especially if you are a writer.

This is particularly true when the stories are rooted firmly in reality. Crimes so lurid, complex, and unlikely that they would be considered overwrought and unbelievable as fiction, become a window into the human condition when they are revealed as fact. Beyond offering the power of a nonfiction narrative, such tales blend extraordinary characters and settings with motives and investigative techniques so driven by improbability and coincidence that the reader can't possibly believe it—except it's true! More than the gritty details of a horrible murder or the sensation of a string of sex crimes, these contradictions capture the very essence of a genre whose appeal has fascinated for centuries.

While some joke that the genre is as old as the story of Cain and Abel in the Bible, modern true crime writing has been popular since the exploits of local murderers became a staple of simple pamphlets in Elizabethan England. The killings were often unspectacular, but the ensuing trials and executions made for popular reading. One—*Murder in the Red Barn*—told the story of a young country girl who was shot and buried by a farmer who had impregnated her. The crime went unresolved until the girl's mother had a dream that recreated the killing and the burial of the body in a corner of the barn. Pressured by the clarity of it, her husband went to the spot and dug up the girl's body, launching a manhunt for the killer that eventually led to his discovery and hanging in London. Touted as "the crime of the century" and portrayed as a melodrama that contrasted the killer's motivations against the manipulations of his victim, it was a bestseller and popular dramatic subject for over a hundred years.

Collections of these "true crime" pamphlets first began appearing in book form with the arrival of John Osborn's three-volume set *Lives of Remarkable Criminals* in 1735. Despite being held together largely by a preachy editorial style biased toward imparting the moral lessons implicit in every case, these anthologies provided a good read and solid sales while reinforcing a sense of justice. But with the publication of George Wilkinson's *Newgate Calendar* forty years later, the genre moved beyond chronicling the cycle of crime and punishment to include the small details of everyday life, introducing the element of a physical setting to enhance the depth of the story. For the first time, crime writing began to provide all sorts of vital information on the type of clothes, food, drink, transportation, speech, and manners of the day. Beyond bringing the events to life, this stylistic shift added a new dimension by introducing layers of detail that captured the essence of an era's social fabric in a way that formal history books rarely bothered with.

By the end of the 1800s, these basic stories revealed a far larger trend—that the nature of crime had begun to change alongside shifts in society. Before, most crimes had been economic in origin, resulting from poverty, hunger, or desperation. But the onset of the industrial age and the new concept of leisure time was accompanied by a decided change in the temper of crime. The standard fare of assault and murder, even those spectacular cases resulting from rage, passion, or drunkenness that were the highlights of the seventeenth and eighteenth centuries, had given way to more complex crimes. Highway robberies were rampant, police corruption was not uncommon, innocent people were framed, tales of cannibalism were drifting in from the colonies, and sex crimes (mostly rape) were starting to appear with frightening regularity. Book collections of smaller crimes were still popular, but a new publication had taken hold. The tabloid *Illustrated Police News* provided up-to-date coverage along with a new twist—sketches of the hangings, floggings, and beheadings that captivated the public.

As the peasants and farmers began to shift to the cities in search of jobs, the professional criminal emerged just as seemingly "motiveless crimes"—usually acts of brutal violence where there was no apparent link between the killer and the victim—began to appear. Then, on the last day of August in 1888, a spree of killings began in London's Whitechapel district that changed everything. Three months later, five prostitutes were dead, often carved beyond recognition, and police had a murderer on their hands who wrote them notes accompanied by body parts as proof of his handiwork. He called himself "Jack the Ripper."

Although the term "serial killer" wouldn't be coined for another century, the newspapers trumpeted the story and fear settled over the entire city as dozens of theories emerged. But the killings ended as abruptly as they had begun and the "Ripper" was never caught. In his wake he left a population frightened and fascinated with his motives, methods, and madness. After all, there was no apparent reasoning behind the murders, no robberies or other profit motive, just inexplicable bloodlust. This created a literary and dramatic legacy that has generated a host of books, plays, movies, miniseries, and documentaries ranging from the serious and the scientific to the trashy. But what is most telling is that the "Ripper" has remained a popular topic well into the 1990s.

The inability to solve the "Ripper" murders and the growing tide of dedicated criminals forced the police to adopt new techniques. Although primitive and time-consuming, photography first appeared in London in the form of mug shots. After a British civil servant began using fingerprints to track payments to illiterate pensioners in colonial India, a Scotsman named Henry Faulds introduced the concept to crime fighting in 1880. Twelve years later, Sir Francis Gaulton's book *Fingerprints* created a scientific theory of classification and Scotland Yard was using them to link perpetrators to crimes by 1902. Advances in identifying human blood expanded the growing arsenal of forensic techniques, and cameras were making their way into investigations as a means of recording details at the scene, all of which added another dimension to the way crimes were portrayed in print. For the first time, forensics was starting to play a role in the way true crime was depicted.

The popularity of true crime writing exploded in England with the start of the twentieth century, and America wasn't far behind. In 1910, San Francisco police captain Thomas Duke provided a uniquely American perspective on the previous eighty years of criminal history when he published *Celebrated Criminal Cases of America*. Covering everything from the assassination of Mormon leader Joseph Smith and a wave of anarchist bombings, to the murderous ways of the Plains Indians and the Chinese mobsters in the California gold fields, Duke's classic work provides a portrait of a growing nation with an appetite for violence. As historically important as it was popular, it launched a flood of true crime stories that found a loyal audience in readers of the pulp magazines that first appeared in the 1920s. Available for pennies and printed on low-grade paper, these magazines whetted the public's appetite with all sorts of tales of incredible adventure. With the crime rate rising along with the nation's postwar prosperity, the concept of the old *Illustrated Police News* was adapted to a pulp format and hyped with gruesome photographs of criminals and victims, and pictures of the valiant police at work.

By the 1930s, true crime writing had emerged as a distinct subset of the broad thriller-mystery-suspense genre, usually as a variation on the classic "true detective" magazine. Since the days of frontier justice in the "Wild West" were over, the subjects became more urban and covered everything from bank robbers and bootlegging gangsters to the kidnapping and murder of Charles Lindbergh's nineteen-month-old son. The headlines screamed, the writing was often grossly embroidered and embellished, and the portrayal of the crimes focused on anything that could be made sensational. Whether frowned upon by intellectuals as lowbrow pulp or loved by the working class as a chronicle of the missteps of both the nation's underbelly and elite, true crime writing as a distinct American genre was here to stay.

For the next several decades, true crime had two distinct forms. One was the classic hyperbolic approach complete with lurid pictures; the other was more of a just-the-facts journalism done by hard-boiled reporters. If the case was big enough to merit national attention, a more serious work might emerge in book form after the crime was solved—but it still had to be flashy enough to sell. One of the first crimes to get this treatment was the Lindbergh kidnapping, which produced a number of books by reporters assigned to the story. *In Search of the Lindbergh Baby* implicated Al Capone and floated the theory that young "Buster" Lindbergh was still alive, while *The Trial of Richard Hauptmann* focused on the police investigation and forensic evidence and fueled the debate over whether the final verdict was a just one or even if the true killer had been caught. Later books such as *The Boston Strangler* continued the tradition of adapting hard-driving journalism, one that accepted the premise that if there was a hole in the facts, so be it— that's the way the story would be written rather than stray from the truth. Whether the approach was hyperbolic or straight-edged, the public's impression of true crime writing was largely based on the concept of extreme violence and lurid detail. Then Truman Capote published *In Cold Blood* and everything changed again.

As an established fiction writer who had begun to stray toward journalism, Capote went to Kansas in 1959 to write a magazine article on the murder of a local farmer and his family. But when he turned his talent on a terrible crime in an ordinary place, he changed the entire genre with a single work. *In Cold Blood* was published in 1966 to staggering critical acclaim and dramatic sales. The book combined everything that the classic true crime story had come to embody—the setting, the killers, the victims, the murder, the forensics, the investigation, the arrest, the trial, and the eventual execution of the guilty—but added an entirely new dimension. Using his considerable literary skills and some imagination, Capote managed to climb inside the characters' minds as he recreated the strange coincidences and twisted dynamics that are at the heart of every murder. By applying the narrative techniques of the best fiction with the grim realism of nonfiction reportage, Capote riveted the nation with the twists and turns of his self-named "nonfiction novel." Although there was controversy over the book's blend of "faction" (Capote didn't capture the final scene with brilliant reporting; he created it) and its role in the established literary spectrum, that was a relative footnote to the unprecedented level of publicity and success that it achieved. Capote seemed to be everywhere.

His face peered out from the covers of *Newsweek* and the *New York Times Book Review*; feature stories about the book dominated the national magazine market for months, television and radio shows focused on the author, and Hollywood came calling for the movie rights. *In Cold Blood* attracted readers, inspired other writers, and encouraged publishers to reconsider the genre as something more than a down-market fascination with blood and gore, effectively launching the modern era of true crime writing.

It didn't take long to see the impact. The 1970s started with the madness of the Manson Family killings in Los Angeles and ended with the arrest of Ted Bundy after his swath of sex murders cut across America from Seattle to Florida. The old form of a motiveless killing that had emerged nearly a hundred years earlier had now taken on bizarre twists that encompassed everything from drug cults and mind control to bizarre sex acts and necrophilic trophies. The term "serial killer" was being used to cover a class of individuals who repeatedly murdered and mutilated, often acting out strange scenarios, taking body parts, or posing victims for the police to find. Baffled and pressured by the public to explain this depravity, the FBI set up its Behavioral Science Unit in Quantico, Virginia in the mid-1970s to create psychological profiles and develop motivational theories of the killers. As always, people were terrified and fascinated with the horror of the incidents, but the physical or investigative details were no longer enough—readers now wanted to know the *why* behind this kind of crime.

To meet this demand, a new style of writing emerged that lay beyond the bounds of the old-fashioned "who-dunit" approach to crime reporting. Inspired by Capote and more literary in tone and scope, these proponents of what Tom Wolfe called "The New Journalism" applied fiction techniques to their work. The classic who-what-where-when-why-how limits of the past started to give way to books that offered vivid characters, symbolism, metaphor, rising conflict, and a well-paced plot in addition to a story about a horrible crime. While Capote's genius had raised what had been a subgenre of the far more popular thriller-mystery-suspense-detective class to the level of literature, books like *Helter Skelter*, *The Only Living Witness*, and *The Stranger Beside Me* displayed the ability to take a criminal situation and offer readers a sense of resonance to all areas of life.

Over the next decade, true crime quickly grew into one of the most popular of all nonfiction genres. The quality of writing in books such as *The Hillside Strangler, Son, Fatal Vision, The Mormon Murders, In Broad Daylight, Masquerade,* and many others drew in the public, climbed the bestseller lists, and eventually reached broader audiences through TV miniseries and feature films. Some crimes drew major headlines, but others seemed to come out of nowhere until the book arrived. Always a cyclical business, the publishing industry jumped on the trend and authors such as Jack Olsen,

Ann Rule, and Joe McGinness were heavily promoted. Crimes seemed to become wilder as the Jeffery Dahlmer, John Wayne Gacy, and Richard Ramirez cases grabbed the headlines and dominated the airwaves. Media attention was up, but only a book could take the reader into the depths of the investigation and the grim details of the murders.

By the early 1990s, true crime sales were at a fever pitch and several trends had clearly emerged. On one hand, there were ambitious books backed by years of research as writers like Lowell Cauffiel, Harry MacLean, and Darcy O'Brien used the form to expose the corners of American culture while managing to keep the reader glued to the page. On the other were the "insta-books" that popped out as a response to the public's immediate interest in a case. Some of these were credible efforts that matched the speed of magazine coverage but provided more depth, detail, and photographic coverage than any magazine or newspaper could afford to match. Others were little more than a mix of clipped news articles, excerpts from the trial transcript, a few police photos, and details from weather reports all bound by a spine. Driven by the public's curiosity and made possible by advances in printing and production technology, these books put a dent in the market for feature-oriented true crime magazine pieces. Since they required just a few weeks, these quickies also siphoned off interest from more serious works that took several years to produce. Many saw insta-books as a throwback to the less serious aspects of the genre's pulp past. But their success was undeniable. *The Milwaukee Murders,* which covered the Jeffery Dahlmer case, and several books on the O.J. Simpson trial—including Simpson's own *I Want To Tell You*—landed on the national bestseller lists. No matter what approach an author took, true crime was hot enough to make everything sell.

Since nothing breeds imitation like success, the appeal of the form began to surface in other areas. Traditional mystery fiction began to adopt elements that had been the province of true crime by incorporating massive amounts of factual detail about police procedures, forensic science, criminal psychology, and judicial practices to flesh out scenes and drive plots. Movies such as *Silence of the Lambs* wrapped fact and fiction around the figure of a serial killer in a way that captivated audiences and spawned television shows such as *Profiler.* Tabloid TV wasn't far behind, trumpeting new crimes almost as soon as they happened and tracking the latest developments in cases that had reached the courts. Shows such as *American Journal, Hard Copy,* and *A Current Affair* all provided shallow but continuous coverage that amplified any crime of consequence. Before long, reality-based programming became the order of the day as *Cops, Rescue 911, Adventures of the Highway Patrol,* and a host of similar shows did much the same for drunk driving, petty drug busts, car thefts—everyday crimes of no real significance.

While the growing media attention over the last few years has helped drive a broader awareness of true crime as quickly as it fed the public's seemingly insatiable appetite for it, it has also created a schism in the genre. On the low end there are the insta-books that often focus on the aspects of the media coverage that make every story sensational. Although popular and successful, they can often gloss over the motivational factors that make a crime compelling and interesting. Since the books are frequently written by young journalists crossing over from a story they have been covering, and marketed as paperback originals, advances tend to be low, and un-agented contracts often yield low royalty rates as well. The resulting lack of money can discourage writers from continuing in true crime, particularly those who get pigeonholed by publishers as authors of insta-books—a label that can create problems when it comes to future projects.

At the other end of the spectrum, serious works of literary merit have continued the trend of solidly researched, evocatively written journalism that represents the best that true crime writing has to offer. Books like the 1997 Edgar Winner *Power to Hurt* by Darcy O'Brien, the 1996 Edgar Winner *Circumstantial Evidence* by Pete Earley, the widely praised *All God's Children* by former *New York Times* reporter Fox Butterfield, *Trespasses* by Howard Swindle, and *Two by Two* by Jim Schutze all signal a resurgence of work that can go head-to-head with the power and appeal of masterful fiction.

The popularity of true crime has endured because it is that rare genre that offers many things to many people.

On one level, its lurid depictions of bizarre acts and its quick-paced narratives provide thrills by shocking and titillating people even as it draws them into a world that lies outside their normal experience. On another, it safely opens up the dark side of human nature that everyone acknowledges, but few are willing to explore. In either case, it sells.

Chapter Two

STRANGER THAN FICTION

Finding a Story That Sells

Despite FBI statistics indicating a dramatic drop in crime across America in the 1990s, true crime writers are not experiencing any shortage of material. In 1996 alone, there were over twenty thousand murders and nearly 1.8 million violent crimes (murder, rape, robbery, and aggravated assault) nationwide. But there is a huge difference between a crime such as "Husband Kills Cheating Wife" or "Man Shot at Bank Machine" and one that people want to learn more about. Even then, what can initially appear to be a sensational story of murder—even a truly heinous one—does not automatically translate into an article, book, or screenplay that someone will buy.

Everything starts with picking the right crime, one that is complex and compelling enough to merit both your own commitment and a publisher or producer's interest. As former Chicago policewoman and longtime true crime writer Jay Fletcher is fond of saying, "No matter how bad the crime was or how bad the criminal was, describing the crime itself only takes four pages. So what do you do with the other four hundred?" In other words, the case cannot be a two-dimensional affair where motive and action are clearly linked. Those "other four hundred" pages are where the real story lies and you'll have to choose it carefully. Factors such as access to information and sources, competition with other writers and media outlets, the amount of time and money it will take, and even the geographic location of the crime must all be considered before undertaking any project.

The Classic Case

While the catchall phrase "true crime" can often be interpreted to cover a variety of sensational violations of the penal code, the truth is that the majority of projects sold deal almost exclusively with an unusual murder. This has been true since *Helter Skelter* and *The Stranger Beside Me* pushed the Manson and Bundy cases into the mainstream nearly twenty years ago. These days, crimes that involve Wall Street financiers who bilk others out of millions or Mafia families who run brutal syndicates are not generally considered to be true crime material; they are regarded as "high finance" or "mob" stories that appeal to a different type of audience. Even the sixty-plus books on the most recent "crime of the century," the O.J. Simpson double-murder case, have come to be regarded as falling in the "true law" category. As Charles Spicer, the editor responsible for St. Martin's True Crime Library, says, "True crime has to have a murder someplace. There has to be a body and the more twisted the motivation of the killer, the more fascinating the case. People are mesmerized by the extremes of human character and murder brings those elements out like nothing else."

But a run-of-the-mill murder case won't capture attention in a way that would lead people to spend money to learn more about it. Simply put, a lot of the news that is reported in the papers and on TV is bad and overwhelms the average person, and a large percentage of the population becomes callused when it comes to crime news. The result of this tabloidization of the general news media is that it takes something spectacular to get the public's attention, something so unexplainable that people find themselves stopping to ask "how could they do that?" Reading a classic true crime story is a lot like witnessing a car accident—it's so terrible that you can't bear to watch, yet so fascinating that you can't stop looking at it.

Although murder is the name of the game, the ideal crime for a prospective writer is usually one that has already been solved. Known in legal parlance as *closed cases,* these are crimes where a suspect has been arrested, tried, convicted, and sentenced. Some writers will follow a case as it develops and winds its way through the court system, but these stories are far trickier to sell unless you have an established track record in the genre. "You need to have a conviction when you're trying to sell a story. It really doesn't work without one," says Paul Dinas, who edits the popular Zebra True Crime imprint for Kensington. "We have a conviction clause that says if the accused is not convicted of the crime, we have the choice to cancel the book. This is primarily for legal reasons, because you can't have a person accused of killing someone only to get away. But closure is very important in true crime because readers don't want to be left hanging, they want to know the system works, that this kind of behavior won't be tolerated, and that, in some way, they are protected from it."

While this may seem overly cautious, statistics indicate that a significant number of murder cases go unsolved. Whether due to lack of evidence, cutbacks in police budgets and staff, or the fact that most prosecutors are keenly aware of their conviction rates and tend to pursue cases that they are sure they can win, it is a fact that many killers go unapprehended or escape conviction. For writers, the risk is that a typical murder case can take years to prosecute. This can chew up an advance without any guarantee that there will be a solid ending to the case.

The only exception to this rule surfaces in the form of the popular insta-books. Publishers who wait for a conviction can find themselves beaten to the market by a project that focuses on the crime, the investigation, and an arrest of the suspect without waiting for a trial. These projects are far more difficult to do for both legal and narrative reasons, but often the hype from the media will create an opening in the marketplace for something that provides more depth than an article or a short segment on the evening news. The product will not be as conclusive or in-depth as a book done after the fact, but it will fill a niche by providing a level of information that hasn't been available. Plus the ongoing media buzz offers a built-in level of publicity that no marketing campaign can match, and some publishers are loath to miss an opportunity if there is enough material in hand.

"A conviction is preferable, but I don't think you absolutely need to have one to do a true crime book," says St. Martin's Spicer. "We've done a lot of insta-books and have come to dominate that part of the market. The book we did on the Susan Smith case, *Sins of the Mother*, stands on its own merit and our book on the Dahlmer case was a very big seller. You have to have an arrest, but sometimes you just can't wait for the trial."

Fascinating murders and convictions aside, the heart of any true crime story lies in the characters and settings that surround it. Something has to set this series of events apart from the twenty other crimes that are reported in the paper every week and people have to be able to identify with the individuals who are involved—the victims, their family, the detectives, or the legal team. As Jack Olsen, the man many refer to as "the dean of modern true crime writing," explains, "My emphasis is always on what made the criminal a criminal, to explain where the criminal came from and what the family dynamic was, what the background was, to give you an idea of how they became that way. The human relations is where the story is. It's not just the crime, it's all in the background dynamics because if you have a great crime and lousy characters, people don't want to know about it."

In some cases, the dichotomy of what things appear to be and what they really are—the unveiling of a secret life or discovering an unspeakable crime in a town that is an icon for the American dream—can only be explained within the context of a time and place. A setting frames and often explains the motives of a story's characters in subtle ways that can inform and entertain while also highlighting the odd sense of coincidence that can tie victims and criminals together. In many cases, it often reflects a larger theme that deals with fundamental truth about society and humanity. Darcy O'Brien, author of the bestseller *Two of a Kind: The Hillside Stranglers,* believes that the setting is essential in putting a brutal crime in perspective. "I'm interested in moral, legal, and social questions surrounding the cases I cover. It's never the crime *per se*, although there may be an interesting psychological angle, but what surrounds it, what makes it possible socially and historically. No one can comprehend of how these people are capable of extreme behavior like this, no one can explain the sadism, the sexual component, or the 'scientific' element of seeing how long it took someone to die. But the circumstances around a crime can help others to see how it happened."

Beyond the unusual and the interesting, a great true crime case is always instructive. It allows people to see beyond the tragedy at the surface and gain an understanding of a world that is foreign to them. Sometimes this is revealed through a clash between layers of society; other times it is a conflict between generations of a family or a set of fundamental drives—greed, sex, or violence—that have gone out of control. When a good writer takes a reader beyond the violence and delves into the underlying motives that have created it, certain truths are revealed that are bigger than the story itself. Capote's *In Cold Blood* took the kind of crime that typically appears as a three-inch blurb buried in the back of a paper—an unknown Kansas family murdered by two drifters—and transformed it into a work that illuminated the entire spectrum of the human condition. At its best, true crime can offer a range of insights into the psychology of an entire society.

"These days you can read about crime everywhere or see it on a TV show any night of the week. There are a hundred venues for people to get information from and, as publishers, we have to be grateful that there are still people who like to get it from books," explains Michaela

Hamilton of Putnam/Penguin. "But one of the big problems with a book in this environment is timeliness. By the time we can publish a book it's not news any more, so it has to provide something else, something new. The true crime writer has to be able to offer something beyond the headlines. That's what I look for and that's what a reader looks for and it can't be a cut-and-paste job like an insta-book—there has to be a level of depth and complexity or a completely new angle that no one has been able to bring to the coverage before. That's why people read true crime."

The First of Many Sources

An unusual murder. A conviction. A cast of unusual characters. An interesting setting. A universal message. Even when the parameters of a good story are known, finding one that fits them is a continual challenge. But if only a small percentage of the twenty thousand murders each year fit the basic criteria for a true crime story, there still would be thousands to choose from. While there is plenty of opportunity for everyone, the secret is in knowing where to look.

The logical place to start is the local newspaper. Papers are terrific places to look for ideas, particularly in the metro section of a big daily where crimes are first reported. Unless the slaying is particularly notable, the first mention of a case will often appear as a small news story bearing just the facts of a case and then will be followed by a series of stories as the crime unfolds. If you live in a large city, most dailies also carry what are known as *zone* sections that target outlying suburbs. Inserted in the regular edition instead of the main metro section to provide readers with more specific local coverage, zones are good for leads because the crime reporting tends to be more in-depth than the city edition simply due to less competition. If a doctor were gunned down on a New York City street, it might merit two paragraphs on page six of the metro section; the same act in a suburb would run on the cover of the zone section.

Often a paper will run a regional roundup section in a Sunday edition that will condense coverage from all the zone editions of the past week. These pieces tend to be shorter, but they can easily be traced back to the original through a phone call or a trip to the library. Libraries are also great places to review out-of-town papers that can yield an interesting prospect. In every case, it is important to clip or copy, date, and file any interesting stories and review them regularly. This may seem like an unscientific way of separating the wheat from the chaff, but the simple fact is that great crime stories do not appear every week. Dogged persistence is the fundamental trait of a true crime writer and, with practice, you will be able to distinguish a good story from the countless routine felonies.

While a paper will often produce the kernel of a potential story idea, the downside is that a thorough review of multiple editions is often time-consuming. The key word here is "thorough" because many times a story will first surface as a small piece no longer than a few paragraphs. To compensate, a number of established writers have turned to their computers for help. "The place where you find stuff is by looking at newspaper databases and I use the Internet to look at stories," says Fred Rosen, author of the paperback classic *Lobster Boy* and a number of other works. "Every day, I'll go through a couple of papers and if something interests me I'll download it and look at it later. These days, I look for something that will be a good read and stories that I think I can get behind and get to the motivation that the reporter didn't have time to bring out. I want to create a setting that gives some order to the universe, some sense of explanation about how these horrible things came to pass. It takes time, but after awhile you develop an 'eye' for what works and what doesn't. The first thing I'd tell someone is 'go to AP wire and look around.'"

While newspapers are good sources for breaking news, city and regional magazines are often good bets for leads on stories that are more developed. Magazines like *Southern Exposure, Alaska, Yankee, Georgia Magazine, Chicago, Boston, Los Angeles, Springfield!* (Missouri), and *Willamette Week* (Oregon) all feature extensive local stories that go beyond daily coverage but rarely exceed five thousand words—enough to give you a solid idea of what elements are present. The only cautionary note with using a magazine piece as a source is that it may not be strong enough to merit a book. As Scott Anderson, author of *The 4 O'clock Murders,* explains, "These days, the market for true crime won't support a book or screenplay about a basic crime or even an uninteresting serial killer unless there is a larger message contained in the story—something universal that speaks to people who would never do something like this; something in the background that speaks to a more common human condition that adds a dimension. If it doesn't have that, then it's just an article and not a larger project. The bottom line is that just because something is a great magazine piece does not mean that there's a book there. This and the issue of how resolved the case is are the two things I look at right away when considering a story."

National magazines like *People* and tabloids like the *Enquirer, Globe,* or *Star* are less fertile sources, but shouldn't be overlooked. *People's* coverage can often highlight a regional case that you might have missed, one that was not brash enough to merit overexposure on *Hard Copy* or *A Current Affair* but still might have potential. Despite criticism from mainstream journalists over the practice of paying sources for information, the tabloids have gained a greater degree of stature for their scoops in the Simpson and JonBenet Ramsey murder cases, and some of their smaller crime pieces are wild enough to merit a second look.

Another effective tactic is to let distant friends and relatives know that you are in the market for offbeat crime stories. People often take a perverse pride in unusual local events and are quick to clip articles and forward them along. Should you decide to follow through on a case, your network might also be able to provide personal insights or connections to background sources. In many cases, this approach can extend your reach into small towns in out-of-the-way locations that you would have otherwise missed while taking almost no time or effort on your part.

Closer to home, word of mouth can be a very powerful medium; keeping people aware that you are on the lookout for crime stories can yield a range of results. Police patrolling a beat, detectives, prosecutors, and local reporters are all sources of information about crimes that you might not have heard about. They can also provide a quick check on a few facts you have come across when exploring a case's potential. For established writers, editors and agents often come up with possible stories. Most editors keep a file on interesting crimes and agents are always keeping an eye open for a project that might suit a client, but that doesn't always mean that it's right for the writer. "I routinely look through newspapers and magazines, but my agent will call me with an idea he's heard or come across in something I haven't read," says Harry MacLean, a former attorney and judge whose first book, *In Broad Daylight*, won an Edgar, landed on the *New York Times* bestseller list, and was made into a film. "Sometimes an editor will get in touch about a possible project, but I've always found them to be lousy ideas. Just because it's an instantly graspable 'high concept' story that has good marketing potential doesn't mean it's going to be an interesting book at all. In many cases, it's just deep enough to be a magazine article."

The latest source of story ideas is the Internet. Both America OnLine (AOL) and CompuServe have popular sites that contain chat rooms, offer online symposiums, and provide access to newsgroups such as Alt.True Crime where people share ideas, opinions and tips. Compu-Serve's True Crime Forum attracts a lot of attention from leading writers such as Jack Olsen and Ann Rule, who schedule sessions to answer questions, and AOL has a true crime section in The Book Report (TBR). The Alt.True Crime and Alt.Crime newsgroups have a lot of information, but are highly unfocused and can be time-consuming to wade through.

Outside of the popular online services, The Crime Writer is a Web site sponsored by Satore Township and is an excellent jumping-off point that offers dozens of links. These include everything from short summaries of the day's crimes to the latest-breaking news from Court TV and separate pages for writers' resources, news, research tools, and authors and publications. Yahoo's crime page delivers a valuable index of crime-related sites on the Web that is updated continuously, providing quick access to pages by the FBI and Prison Resources, various forensic pages, and a over a dozen online chat rooms for writers interested in the genre. While new pages are coming online each day, a recent search based on the key words "true crime" resulted in over five thousand site descriptions of related material. These ranged from The United Kingdom Police and Forensics page and Cop Net (with access to city, county, state, and a number of federal law enforcement agencies) to more obscure locales such as "Brian's Basement: True Crime."

While informative and entertaining, the current downside of the Internet is its sprawling randomness. Most writers who use it for story prospecting have a number of sites that they visit on a regular basis and a second tier that they will use to do background research. Many create their own search strings on different topics (murder, serial killer, and so on) just to see what comes up, and then maintain a list of the more interesting pages, but this can eat up a lot of time and produce limited results. But if you are a savvy computer user, the Net can be a valuable resource when you are looking for a story.

Getting Started

Even when you know what you are looking for, finding the right true crime case is still far from a scientific process. Stories are often deeply personal for writers—and any crime, if it resonates and connects to a vision you have for it, might be yours to work with. "I don't have a set of criteria about what I'd like to work on, so I listen to everybody tell me about everything," says Jay Fletcher. "But when a spark hits, it's sort of like the weird attraction that happens between people. You get the feeling that 'Hmm, that's one I'd like to know better.' There's a strange sort of magnetism that happens between a writer and their story that's hard to explain, but it's a feeling every writer knows."

Sometimes it's a crime that touches upon something in your past or an area that you've always been fascinated with, but had never taken the time to explore. For many writers it can be a simple but piercing unanswered question, one that embodies the same sense of mystery that they will eventually impart to readers. For others it is an identification with one or more of the characters involved. Most successful true crime writers are quick to admit that they had an interest in a heroic figure, an unsung detective or a brave prosecutor, or even in the intelligence of the criminal. While this last point may seem odd, consider that the majority of criminals featured in true crime books are not ordinary burglars; they are frequently smooth-talking, charming, highly manipulative psychopaths who know how to cover their tracks. But that is what can make a story so interesting. The characters whose surface appearance is so at odds with the crimes they are committing are the ones that rivet people's attention by drawing them into a search for an explanation of their behavior.

As one of the most successful true crime writers of all time, Ann Rule knows what she's looking for in a story. "I go through over three hundred cases before I pick one. I'm not looking for the high-profile case as much as I'm looking for a protagonist, either male or female, that has certain qualities—physical attractiveness, education, money, charisma, charm, success. Those are all the things that people want in their own lives and they always make the reader wonder 'Hey, they had it all—how could they do that? How could they throw it all away?' I'm also looking for a case that is so convoluted that the story will carry itself, a story where just when you think it's run out of turns to take, the characters do something else. When I find the right case the hairs stand up on the back of my neck."

But even when you locate a story you can connect with, you need to make sure it is feasible. In most cases, you will have the basics of the story—a brief description of the crime, the perpetrator, and the victims—and an innate sense that it might be worth pursuing. But just because a story interests you doesn't mean that it is one that you will be willing to commit months, maybe years, to pursuing.

The first step is to conduct some basic preliminary research. This typically begins with a round of phone calls. If the lead came from a newspaper, the reporter who wrote the story is a logical place to start because time or space constraints may have limited the amount of information that made it onto the page. Reporters are also good for quick leads to other players in the case, often supplying phone numbers for the investigating detectives and prosecutors. A trip to the library or a database search on the Internet can produce any related articles that may have been published and can help determine whether the crime is local or one that is just another in a series of events that crosses state lines.

If this effort confirms your instincts, it will be worth the time to visit the people you have talked to and to explore some of the settings involved. While phone calls can provide all sorts of information, there is nothing like getting a fix on the characters involved to determine whether they have enough dynamism and inherent interest to carry a story. These meetings might cover days or be as simple as sharing a cup of coffee or a drink in a favorite bar, but they can generate all sorts of realizations that you would never get over the phone.

"Since I usually spend two or more years on a book, I've got to do between two and three months of preliminary research before I'll start to do a story, before I'll make the decision to get completely involved," Jack Olsen says. "That may sound like a lot, but it is crucial to the success of a project. I once spent six months in New York City looking into a case where a federal Alcohol Tobacco and Firearms (ATF) agent was accused of a series of horrible rapes. He was innocent and the case was fascinating, but he was an asshole and I couldn't write the book because he was an unsympathetic character—both for me to work with and for the reader. I just knew I couldn't make it fly. Conversely, I started a book that became *Salt of the Earth* on a local kidnapping that took place thirty miles from me. It was a small crime, it was local, and my initial interest was fairly casual, but then I met the mother of the victim and she was an amazing person, an incredible survivor, and that changed everything for me. If I hadn't run across her and discovered what a special woman she was, I wouldn't have done the book."

A primary benefit of this research is that you can get an accurate fix on how developed the story is. It is important to avoid stories that are unfolding because you can get frozen out by everything from competition from daily reporters to a lack of access to information tied up by the courts. As a rule, the more uncertain the outcome of a case is, the more frustrated you will be in pursuing it. Local reporters will be pushing for scoops and national stories have a glare to them that makes it difficult to compete unless you have a lot of money and resources. When a story is winding through the court systems, everyone involved has lawyers and is harder to get to, so you need to have some sort of resolution before the flow of information opens up. The bottom line is that you can follow a story while it's unfolding, but you won't get the really good information until it's over.

Another issue to consider is the geographic location of a case. This may seem to be a minor point, but investigative research is a time-consuming process and distance can be a limiting factor. Travel, hotels, food, and the inevitable entertainment expenses involved in getting sources to talk can chew up money at an incredible rate. Crime sprees that cover multiple states multiply the impact of this factor considerably and complicate the issue of access. While techniques differ, most successful true crime writers practice a form of immersive research that involves a lot of hanging around the various players in the case. As people become familiar with your presence, they tend to relax; relationships develop and information comes out. Ideally, you can arrange a number of interviews in advance, but once a line of information surfaces it can take days or weeks to trace it to the end. The quality of a true crime piece depends heavily on the amount of research that goes into it and it is not uncommon to talk to hundreds of people. But if the crime is located on the other side of the country or in three different states, it is difficult to build deeper connections or to react quickly to new developments.

"I live in Colorado, but my second book was in California so I had to go there to do it because you can't immerse yourself in a case unless you're there all the time," says Harry MacLean. "A lot of it involves hanging around with people on nights and weekends. The problem is there's a lot you don't know and the question is how do you deal with that? My way is to just be there, spend time with people, and see what happens. A lot of the big breaks I've got happened just because of that, because I was there when someone was ready to talk. It's always people who make the story work, make it come alive, and you can't get that over the phone or via e-mail. It's expensive, but it's the only way you can do it."

Since this approach can quickly eat up an advance, many writers tend to focus on stories that are more regional in location. This keeps expenses down and allows them to build relationships with detectives and attorneys that might lead to another case down the line. It also offers the advantage of having established insights into the history and resources of an area that an outsider might overlook. All these factors make regional stories the safest bets for first-time writers. But if you think that there aren't any interesting crimes near your home, consider this: Jay Fletcher wrote over a hundred magazine stories about crimes in Chicago and Ann Rule wrote nearly fifteen hundred about crimes in the Northwest—all before they wrote their first books.

When There's Competition

Even though there are far more crimes than writers devoted to them, it is not uncommon to arrive on a scene only to find that there are others already there. This is particularly true when it is a national case that has attracted significant media attention.

All but a handful of writers find it impossible to compete with the resources of television shows such as *Hardcopy, A Current Affair,* or *American Journal*—or the major tabloids. While their bias toward the case tilts their coverage toward the shallow and sensationalistic, the level of competition between them doesn't put a damper on what they are willing to spend to secure rights to a person's story. All too often, writers find themselves in the middle of a huge dog and pony show where everyone has a lawyer "representing" their story. The increased scrutiny makes the police much more tight-lipped and everyone seems to want to get paid for whatever they know.

This is particularly true when the crime takes place in a smaller city or town where people and officials are not used to dealing with the intensity of a media onslaught. The deluge of movies and television shows that carry the "based on a true story" tag line has heightened the nation's overall awareness that there is money to be made off seemingly mundane information, and that has changed the way people treat writers. Within the last two years, a handful of aggressive true crime writers have adopted the practice of securing rights to different versions of the story before anyone else can get to them. While the majority of writers are adamantly opposed to paying for information and some states have "Son of Sam" laws to prevent criminals from profiting from their crimes, these agreements typically promise some amount of compensation "if and when" a film based on the story is made. Since many stories are optioned as films but very few are made, this provides a degree of insulation against the competition while not tapping into advance money for a book or the option fee a writer will receive. In the event that a film or miniseries does make it into production, the writer simply adds the amount promised on top of the fee for the rights.

As much as media interest can heighten the profile of a case and drive the public's appetite for information about it, most writers find it to be a double-edged sword.

"The national media sucks up the interest like a sponge and wears out public interest in it," says Harry MacLean. "I mean, a good book takes two years to produce and who wants to spend $29.95 on a book they think they know everything about? It's harder to sell a classic true crime book as result. Media people can gloss over the facts in pursuit of a certain angle that plays well for them. They throw money around and sign sources up to exclusive releases, misquote people, and can really 'contaminate' the scene of the crime. It's gotten so bad in the last three or four years that I make a point of staying away from the bigger stories."

This scrutiny is another reason most writers wait for closure on a case. The appetite for the latest news quickly siphons off interest as shows, magazines, and insta-books move on to the next big crime. The local reporters will stay with it, but usually on a follow-up basis. Still, even though the pressure of being scooped by three or six other writers is off, that doesn't mean that you will be the only one pursuing the story.

When that happens, you have to make a judgment call. In some cases, a publisher will make it for you. When editors decide that the competition is too steep, that a newcomer is trying to break in against a writer who has a list of bestsellers already, they may offer a kill fee. Typically, a true crime story sells on the merits of the case rather than the writer. But if the other writer is an Ann Rule or a Jack Olsen, with a $250,000 advance and a reputation that buys instant credibility with the authorities, the publisher may believe that the book will never sell against such stiff competition and that it's worthwhile to pay a percentage of the advance to cancel the project. This practice and the percentage offered varies widely between houses.

In most cases, the decision is left up to you. Sometimes you can simply outlast the competition, but any preliminary research effort should look at who the competition is. Be sure to determine whether the other writer is a real threat with a track record and a contract in hand, and not a rumor or someone who has an interest but no credibility. But if there is someone else involved, take the threat seriously—a story has to be very special for several projects to succeed.

"Other writers always complicate the decision to go ahead with a story," Ann Rule explains. "When I wrote *The Stranger Beside Me*, I had to go to Florida to cover Bundy's trial on an advance of $10,000 and I didn't realize that there were three other people writing books on him until I got there. I was discouraged but determined and I said to myself, 'Well, I'll just do the best I can with this' and it outsold the rest of them. I often run across other writers on a story, but many times their projects never materialize. So if you're scared off because someone else says they're going to do it you'll never write anything. But if you go ahead, you have to be sure to come up with something different from the others."

Access

Once you have decided the story has merit, is affordable to do, and free of competition, the final step is determining the level of access you can get to the people and information surrounding it. In addition to the criminal and the victim's family, there are friends, neighbors, and co-workers on both sides, plus defense lawyers, prosecutors, and police to be interviewed. Initial phone calls and visits will give you an idea of how cooperative these sources might be, but their number will surely expand as your research progresses. Once a case is closed, primary material such as court transcripts, police reports, and some evidence will be available, most of which include new names and leads to run down. But willingness to talk is a big variable. Detectives are often barred by commanding officers; the victim's family is often reluctant to go through all the pain and sorrow yet another time, and criminals can be elusive and manipulative in the way they deal with you. Everyone has a different agenda—and, if the case has had any media coverage, people may have had their stories distorted and be even more reluctant to talk. Wearing down resistance through sheer persistence and determination is one tactic that works well, but access often depends on the way in which you are perceived.

"I always sell myself to a lot of the key people as the guy who would tell their story at the highest standard of accuracy," says Lowell Cauffiel, author of *Masquerade* and *Eye of the Beholder*. "I would point out that other writers would just spend two months on a project and I was going to spend two years. If I attended a trial, I never sat with the news media and I always wore the best clothes possible because my objective was to get close to the defense and prosecution and the judge. I wanted to enter their world, so I dressed like an attorney. Plus the news media is often seen as the enemy—both to the criminal and the attorneys—and you need to do something that separates you from the rough and tumble of the news crews. But if I had to interview someone in a working-class bar, I'd wear jeans and a work shirt. People like to talk to people who they think will understand them. I think first impressions are everything and you have to be a chameleon in this type of work."

But there is no guarantee that people will talk. In most cases, you simply write a letter explaining what you are doing and then call as a follow-up to see if they will cooperate. Not everyone will want to be interviewed, but you have to weigh how much access you can get initially against how many people have turned you down. If you can get a number of the significant players to work with you, the chances are that time will wear the other parties down. In many cases, it takes the victim's family a long time before they are willing to deal with the pain of losing a loved one again, but once they are ready it can be both cathartic for them and a wellspring of information for you. Other sources can be slowly backed into talking if only by the reason that everyone else involved has said something and you are giving them a chance to get their version of the story out. But it all takes time and you have to make a judgment call about your chances of success up front.

Once you have found a crime that excites you, one that fills the criteria for a salable piece and you have determined that you can make it happen creatively, financially, and logistically, you're ready to start digging into serious research. Now the real work begins.

Chapter Three

ON THE KILLER'S TRAIL

Research Techniques That Work

All writers can benefit from improving their understanding of where information can be found and enhancing their ability to gather facts quickly. But these skills are the foundation of the true crime writer's investigative approach to every case. At its core, the genre's appeal is based directly on a writer's ability to tell the story behind the story of a criminal event, to explain the forces that created both the motive and the modus operandi of an abnormal act of violence. That requires command of an enormous amount of detail, so as to be able to recreate not only a sequence of events but the mood and setting in which they occurred.

Since many of the answers to the central questions of "why" and "how" can be addressed only by the people

41

involved in the case, a writer often relies on personal contacts and interviews for information. But such primary material can be biased or nonsequential in its presentation and cannot be taken at face value. To effectively frame and interpret such information, it is essential to approach the case with a solid grip on all the background information surrounding it. This requires digging through endless documents, and writers must know both where to look and how to organize a vast number of facts while avoiding any violation of the cardinal rules of accuracy and honesty. To do so takes an open but skeptical frame of mind, a dogged determination to run down every lead, and a solid set of research skills.

"Every time I start a book I'm always terrified that I'll never find out enough because it's often about secrets that people have hidden for years," says Ann Rule. "But I always stay with it and it is amazing what will turn up if you research a case long enough."

When it comes to research, writers must work from the outside in, starting with secondary documents (newspaper stories, magazine articles, video clips, database searches) before moving on to primary documents generated by the legal and judicial systems (police reports, trial transcripts, court records) and then to interviews with personal sources familiar with the case or the lives of the people involved (detectives, lawyers, families, friends, coworkers, neighbors). Finally, the focus tightens on the subject—the criminal.

Naturally, there will be unexpected problems along the way. Secondary source material may be scarce, records missing or inaccurate, authorities uncooperative, or families and friends overprotective and reluctant to talk or share information. But breaks can appear just as quickly. An early article mentions an address, a co-worker divulges a secret no one ever asked about, a phone number gets slipped across a table, a detective offers a quiet hour alone with a box of documents and a Xerox machine. The key is to stay with the chase and have the patience to overcome or outwait every obstacle.

"I try to schedule tasks when I'm researching a book, but once you open up a thread it can take days to run it down," says Lowell Cauffiel. "It's a simple fact that the quality of your true crime book will be directly proportional to the quality of your research. Typically I talk to somewhere between two hundred fifty and five hundred people on a project and my last book was the result of nine to ten shelf-feet of documentation covering everything from court transcripts and police reports to weather reports and psychological profiles. I collect everything when I'm researching and it's amazing what turns up—phone bills, birth certificates, letters between family members, pictures, a lot of stuff that's often seized with a search warrant. It all starts you off on other leads."

This means that everything that comes along relating to a story must be looked at, or at least screened, before being discarded. But even those facts, quotes, and sequences of events that come from reliable sources cannot be taken at face value; all must be verified and cross-checked. Most investigative journalists require at least two sources of confirmation before they will go to print with something, and many editors prefer three.

"If I did research for a straight stretch it would be at least six months on average for a book," Ann Rule adds. "I get everything, all the newspapers, the follow-ups from the cops, input from other reporters on the case who can offer insights that you might not have, everything. I use maps a lot and I have a program in my computer that will give me the topographic nature of the area and the street layout. I also use weather reports and one of my favorite things is to go back to the crime scene and use a timeline book that will help recreate the era. I always go to the place where things will happen so the reader can see it through my eyes. It all adds up. But I try to have three sources for everything. Recently, I got videotapes of the police interrogation from the prosecutors and it made a huge difference, but I still went on to interview the criminal, her husband, and his mistress to confirm certain things."

This all-encompassing approach to research is one of the primary reasons true crime takes so long to write. Unfortunately, quantity generally equates directly to quality when researching a complex story. Leading true crime authors regularly take an average of two years to produce a book, six to eight months of which may be devoted to scouring secondary and primary sources before moving to personal interviews. If a writer decides to follow a case through the courts as it is being decided, scheduling delays and appeals can make the time commitment even longer—and sources are often reluctant to talk about a case that is unresolved.

"You really need to have some sort of resolution occur before you can get a lot of information," says investigative journalist and author Scott Anderson. "You can follow a story while it's unfolding, but it can take forever because there are motions, pretrial hearings, discovery, and appeals and you won't get the really good stuff until it's over and people are willing to talk. But even then, I've found that there's difference between a book and article in the way people deal with you. A book is in the future somewhere and people are much more forthcoming because they're not worried about seeing their words come back at them in week or a month to haunt them. They're just a lot more accessible."

By the time the research phase ends, a solidly executed project will have three primary threads of information that continually cross and confirm each other. One will be from indirect sources, one from direct encounters or documents, and the third from personal interviews. All this material must be assembled in a way that allows individual chronologies to be matched and examined for gaps that may have been missed along the way.

Organization Is the Key

Since any serious research effort will yield a vast amount of information that has been collected from a wide range of sources over a lengthy period of time, establishing a method of effectively organizing material is essential. Few things are more frustrating than not being able to find something you *know* you have—somewhere—when trying to cross-check a fact, and nothing is as lethal as trying to transform several piles of random clippings, notes, transcripts, and photographs into a book. That's why it is important to create a system that works right from the start.

As facts collect and the story begins to build, many writers find it helpful to set aside some time to review material on a weekly basis. A form of informational housekeeping, this approach helps to determine what is valuable, what is missing, and, in many cases, where to look next. This process of continually sifting and evaluating is helpful in several respects. The primary benefit is that it helps prioritize and focus your ongoing research. It also helps to illuminate links between established sources, leads, and facts, and developing information. Something that you may have stumbled across early on but set aside as an interesting dead end may turn out to be significant when placed in the context of other material uncovered later on.

Being organized is also a hallmark of a professional. Investigative research requires an ability to establish trust with a range of individuals—and very few people will trust someone they don't respect. If you come across as a disorganized individual, someone who may be likable but whose methods are suspect, you can often forget about getting people to talk to you. Murder is a serious business and those involved with it expect you to act seriously.

"When I used to approach people for the first time, I always passed out a little package, a self-promotional file that contained a résumé, copies of my best articles, and letters of recommendation," Cauffiel adds. "The letters are from criminals who say I'm a straight-up guy, a recommendation from a victim's family, one from a cop, and one from an attorney. Now I just give them a copy of one of my books because people like to see that I am prepared, that I am willing to give them information with which they can make a decision about talking to me. Preparation and organization are the keys. A lot of journalists are very disorganized when they're doing a story, but I organize everything by colored folders: yellow for victims, red for criminals, blue for police. I also really preliminary research any subject before I make a call to investigate it."

How you physically organize the material—colored folders, different filing cabinets, scanned computer files, or index cards—doesn't matter as much as your dedication to doing it consistently. One of the most effective techniques is to develop chronological timelines for every strand of information you come across. This can be for the crime, the investigation, the people involved and those who were just affiliated with either the criminal or the victim, and the actual physical setting or, with a multistate case, a geographic region. In tracking multiple chronologies, you automatically create a linear progression and sense of order to what would otherwise be an overwhelming deluge of information. In the end, they can be combined to create a master timeline for the story (whether or not it is eventually written that way) and that makes it easy to see the interdependence of facts and actions in what was once a fluid situation. It also shows you where information is missing, a benefit that will be valuable all the way through the first draft.

If all this seems daunting, it can also be helpful to develop a chronology of your efforts through a research log that lists contacts, phone numbers, meeting dates, and sources to serve as an index to the other chronologies. This can also provide a backup if something such as a phone number or address gets misplaced, and it offers an extra measure of protection when it comes time to vet the book for liability issues (see Chapter 6). There's nothing like having a quote along with the date, time, and place of origin in hand when being questioned about its veracity.

One of the most instructive, if overly extensive, uses of the chronological approach to gathering and analyzing information can be seen in the book *Killing Time* by Donald Freed, a prizewinning writer, and Raymond Briggs, a cognitive research scientist. Together, they take all the information surrounding the O.J. Simpson double-murder case—not just the evidence presented in court—and recreate layers and layers of chronologies that raise many new questions. At times, the book's chronologies can seem overwhelming, but they are brilliantly instructive when used as a tool to illustrate how to organize disparate information surrounding a complex crime.

"*Killing Time* went back to an investigation which was botched, looked at alternative theories that were documented but never raised—the drugs and bad elements both the Simpsons were involved in—and then formulated an overall objective analysis by laying out everything in overlapping chronologies," Macmillan editor Mary Ann Lynch explains. "Whether you agree with the verdict or not, this approach changes the paradigm of what happened on the night of the murders. The case wasn't as seamless as it was presented by the prosecution, but it's easy to get carried away with a belief when you don't have all of the information in front of you in a way that allows you to see how it all fits together. *Killing Time* does that in a very powerful way."

Secondary Sources

While all true crime research begins with a tip, a hunch, or a belief, it is always driven by a variety of sources that narrow in scope as the investigation focuses on the primary players—the victims and the criminals. Actual research starts by collecting information from secondary sources, which can include everything from daily and weekly newspapers to magazines and transcripts or tapes of broadcast programs. Since the majority of secondary and primary source material will be generated in the form of a paper trail, it is essential to operate with the belief that information about your chosen subject exists somewhere. It may be in a form or a place you are unfamiliar with, but you must assume that it *does* exist.

This mandate may seem simple, but the primary characteristic of an effective researcher is the belief that information exists and can be tracked down by exercising logic and sheer effort. Every research plan starts by casting a broad net designed to be as inclusive as possible and then tightens as the search progresses. Secondary sources are essential in getting started and can provide valuable background material, but they are most useful when they lead to primary sources.

Most true crime research begins with a preliminary phase based on articles that have already been published about the people or events related to a crime. Beyond catching your interest in a possible subject, these articles are useful for gaining access to reporters who have been covering the case and finding your way to other sources— the name of a detective, witness, neighbor, or co-worker who can be interviewed later, a location, or an address. Early articles are also helpful in providing chronological information about the time and setting of the crime, leads to other circumstances surrounding it, and a sense of whether or not the story is worth pursuing.

"In 1988, four people were murdered in three different locations in Texas in broad daylight and the story went national because of the unusual nature of it. I read about them in a small blurb in the newspaper and I recognized the names of the victims from a book I had read years earlier on a cult operating down there," Scott Anderson explains. "It struck me because the names were unusual, Welsh, and they stuck in my mind. I started calling around to reporters on the *Houston Post* and the Dallas papers and they brought me up to date on a lot of bizarre stuff that had happened since the book was done ten years before. That's when I started to think that there might be a story, because I found that at least twenty people had been killed that the cops knew about and the cult had a death list that they were working their way through."

While preliminary leads in the form of articles and phone calls will help you form an initial opinion about the nature of the crime and the investigation, the perpetrator, and the setting, they can also assist in qualifying another aspect of any potential story. Since ongoing coverage of an investigation often runs into days where there is no breaking news, reporters try to keep the story hot by writing around it with profiles of the victim's family and friends or the investigators attached to the case. Although lack of hard or breaking news can lead many to disregard them as unimportant, these pieces can be critical in deciding whether or not to move forward with a project.

"The preliminary research phase is really important because there are a lot of very sensational crimes that involve unsensational people—people the reader doesn't want to read about—and you have to be very careful about judging who's involved in a case before you commit to a book," Jack Olsen explains. "Say there is a story and the characters are all white trash, well, no one cares. Readers don't like white trash and the book won't sell no matter how great the story is. People don't want to know, they don't want to read about people who are lowlifes and you need to qualify that going in."

One of the big advantages of this type of material is that it can advance—or kill—your effort quickly. Since early articles tend to contain mentions of other sources surrounding a story, a few phone calls or a trip to the library to look for any other published material can rapidly flesh out the basic dimensions of a crime. All libraries will have back issues of local and regional newspapers and national magazines on file and many have subscriptions to out-of-town papers. Print indexes of newspaper articles are available at many libraries or through University Microfilms Inc. in Ann Arbor, Michigan. An increasingly useful source of information is the Internet; many online services provide full reprints of articles and even more links to other sources. Most libraries now have some sort of online search capacity, but anyone with a computer and a modem can take advantage of these resources from home or office.

While the availability of these services can vary from an option provided by a national service supplier such as CompuServe to a contract with major database providers like the Dow Jones News/Retrieval, Knight-Ridder's DIALOG, or LEXIS/NEXIS, they all can drastically cut down the time involved in gathering information. The dedicated database providers usually offer a connection to information gathered by large numbers of organizations in full-text formats rather than abstracts of articles, and some specialize in areas such as TV broadcast transcripts or public records. On the downside, the best of these are not cheap, and complicated searches can be costly. Newspapers that are available through commercial index services include the *Los Angeles Times, Wall Street Journal, Boston Globe, Denver Post, USA Today, San Francisco Chronicle, Washington Post, Christian Science Monitor, New York Times, Houston Post, Atlanta Constitution and Journal, Detroit News, St. Louis Post-Dispatch,* and the *Chicago Tribune,* and there are many others. Many of these papers also have back issues available via computer through in-house services. A full directory of over five thousand databases and hundreds of vendors can be found in *The Directory of OnLine Databases* from Gale Research.

While library and database searches can be helpful in screening cases, a local paper that isn't linked to a service can be hard to beat when it comes to firsthand knowledge and initial leads to other sources. But don't limit the search to articles about the crime; smaller papers have a wealth of what seems to be routine information that can be extremely valuable in re-creating the setting later on. Look at letters to the editor, society columns, police reports, legal notices, weather reports, and obituaries. The latter can be valuable in tracking down extended family members, particularly those with different last names through marriage, or individuals who may seem unconnected with the victim. It is often amazing what can surface.

"There's always something there if you scratch hard enough," explains Edna Buchanan, a Pulitzer Prize-winning reporter who covered over three thousand murders for the *Miami Herald* before becoming a bestselling author. "A lot of writers think that there are things that aren't worth writing about, but a killing has an impact on everyone around the victim, on every life it touches. Then there are the dynamics of how it brought all these people to a place in space and time for it to have happened. There's always something there that's revealing about people and society."

If the crime is in a different geographic region and you're not sure what the local paper is or which papers cover what areas, the *Editor & Publisher International Yearbook* lists daily and weekly papers on a state-by-state, city-by-city basis. It also lists other papers put out by ethnic and interest groups that may contain a different slant or a broader approach to the coverage. Other sources for newspaper listings are *The National Directory of Community Newspapers* and *Bacon's Newspaper Directory.*

Once you have made a commitment to the project, be sure to set aside time to visit the local paper and go through back issues. Older issues may contain small but important nuggets such as marriage announcements, or promotions or records of business openings or failures along with photographs, all of which can help create a historical record. In cases where you can develop a relationship with a reporter or editor, you can often gain access to files that contain unpublished material that may have value; in others you may simply connect with a staff member whose local knowledge can drastically shorten your learning curve.

Beyond the local paper, another frequently overlooked source is a local historical society. These are organizations with files, publications, and members who can help in re-creating a background and setting for the crime. In many cases, the crime will be big news and they will be more than willing to share their information about the local way of life.

"I usually start research by going to the area and finding people who really know about a place, and there's always local historians around and they love to talk about it," says Darcy O'Brien. "They put you on to the right books and other people, so I never go to the library as a start. Once you know what you have to read you can get it via an interlibrary loan at your hometown and the local newspaper is a tremendous place to start. Never underestimate the resources of a local newspaper. I found a small local paper in Kentucky that won two Pulitzers. The people who run these papers are often very literate and literary because it's a labor of love and it is their life's work."

For bigger or more bizarre crimes that capture national attention, magazines can be helpful secondary sources. This is particularly true of regional publications. If you are unfamiliar with the area's glossier magazines, a quick run through a periodicals directory at the library can prove helpful. The *Standard Periodical Directory* from Oxbridge Communications and *Ulrich's Periodicals Directory* are good places to start, but beware—the word "periodical" is far larger than you might think. These directories will include information on everything from popular magazines to obscure newsletters on trade policies, economic trends, and electronics. The good news is that they will usually include a name—usually that of the editor—that can focus your search and make access easier.

Other secondary sources that can be helpful include radio and television broadcasts. Most stations now offer either transcripts or videotapes of each broadcast and the footage, particularly raw news feeds or pieces shot by bystanders with home video cameras, can provide dramatic coverage of breaking news. The Television News

Index and Abstracts service, produced by the Vanderbilt University News Archive in Tennessee, covers ABC's *Nightline,* CNN's *PrimeNews,* and the national news broadcasts from CBS, NBC, and ABC. Public television's *NewsHour with Jim Lehrer* (formerly the *MacNeil-Lehrer News Hour*) is available through a print index and some commercial databases. Journal Graphics in Denver is also an excellent source for transcripts of news shows from around the nation. If something appears in a print record of a show, the next move should be to contact the network or affiliate directly to request a tape of the segment. Visuals vary widely, but they can often prove helpful when you're trying to re-create scenarios down the line.

One of the greatest research assets is the nearest library. While online services are fast and efficient, many local libraries (or those of nearby universities) can provide you with something that no computer can—a librarian. These people, particularly reference librarians, are trained experts who keep up with state-of-the-art information retrieval methods. But be focused in your request for help when you approach them because the majority of information on a subject you think of by one name may be found under a different heading you never thought of. Generally friendly and willing to help you find your way, librarians often know multiple sources on a subject but will only suggest one to save both your time and theirs. For example, if you ask about "the death penalty" you may miss out on the much bigger supply of information filed under "capital punishment" simply because the librarian assumed you knew what you wanted.

If you live in anything larger than a small town, it is important to understand how the library system is structured. In cities, a main library will typically have far greater resources than a satellite branch, and smaller communities may have a limited collection due to a sparse population density and fewer tax dollars. But no library has everything. In the case of recent or breaking news, you may find yourself directed to a computer bulletin board or Usenet group by a librarian. For less time-sensitive materials, a host of new electronic services have upgraded the old-fashioned interlibrary loan system and virtually everything is available if you can wait.

Primary Sources

The real goal of the energy invested in uncovering a solid secondary source is that it will lead you directly to a primary source. These will be records or documents that have been generated by either an individual or an organization that are germane to the victim, the criminal, the crime, or its solution. Primary sources can range from social security numbers and canceled checks to police files or trial transcripts. Once again, it is essential to assume that some record exists and then go about locating it. While the last decade has seen an increasing number of people trying to "move off the grid" and effectively disappear from the hundreds of financial, legal, and regulatory indexes that are part of modern life, the truth is that most Americans would be surprised to learn how much information about them is readily available. Credit cards track spending patterns, phone bills identify contacts and provide timelines, tax records reflect income and assets, and court records contain everything from depositions to lawsuits. When located and pieced together, this material often lets you develop a fairly cohesive story without ever having interviewed a single person.

With the spread of the Internet, even the most private data is available at the push of a button. Information such as home addresses, listed and unlisted phone numbers, and financial data can all be found by using sites like KnowX, InfoSpace, or Find a Friend (as well as countless others that are continually coming online) as a starting point. These sites also provide direct links to other Web sites and sources. One of the best known is the famous yet ironically named Stalker's Home Page. Designed to show users how their privacy can be violated through the use of online databases, this service has become the definitive source of database locations containing personal information and is a good starting point when looking for sources. As strange as it sounds, a thorough research effort can yield a startlingly accurate and detailed portrait of an individual that you have never even seen, let alone met. This can include everything from height, weight, and eye color to a complete medical, financial, and legal history.

If someone has been in the military, or has studied or taught at a university that uses social security numbers for identification, or has a listed telephone number, the chances are that they can be tracked down on the Web by someone who knows only that fact about them. Not the number itself, just the fact that they were in the service or in college or have a phone.

Take the phone number as an example. If you were to go to the Internet and type InfoSpace into a popular search engine such as HotBot or AltaVista, you would be confronted by a menu of options. If you clicked onto the InfoSpace People Search Directory, you would be able to access the home addresses of the 112 million people in the United States with listed phone numbers. Type in the name of someone you are looking for and a map of their neighborhood appears with an X marking their residence. Not good with maps? Then click on an icon and specific directions to get there will slide out of your printer.

This can be done by anyone with a computer and a little time and desire, but it is just the start of what is possible. If you are really looking into someone's past, there are a number of database services that will charge a fee but will provide highly detailed data on specific aspects of a person's life. This can include social security numbers, driving records, court records, real estate holdings, liens, divorce petitions, even the names of U.S. companies registered in Switzerland.

Privacy issues aside, the advantage a primary source offers is that documents cannot talk back or evade what is in them. But that doesn't mean they are always absolute or infallible. They can lie or unintentionally mislead because they were prepared by another human being. Just as everything can be found, so it must be checked. As always, the trick is knowing where to look, and every true crime writer needs a basic but solid understanding of how both the police and court systems work to be able to access records that will help tell a story.

The Police

As both Court TV and the nationally televised proceedings of the Simpson double-murder trial revealed, the pace of the investigative and judicial processes is a far cry from what most people have come to expect. Unlike television dramas that have murders discovered and criminals convicted within the space of an hour's episode, the real world is filled with serpentine twists, lapses in logic, and endless bureaucratic delays. What appears to be an easy crime to solve can often dissolve into an outright acquittal in the face of crafty defense strategies or the most minor of legal technicalities. In many instances, the limits of justice are revealed in a harsh manner.

"There are plenty of cases where I know who did the murder, the cops know, the victim's family knows, but the prosecutor's office won't file charges because they don't have enough evidence," Edna Buchanan explains. "That's why true crime is deceiving as a genre, because most cases don't get solved. Prosecutors are very aware of their conviction rates and they like a sealed case, one with a smoking gun *and* a signed confession, before they will take it to court. How often does that happen? So a lot of cases just never get prosecuted and the murderer walks free because smart criminals don't leave smoking guns or sign confessions. People like to think the system works and they often look to true crime to reassure them, but it really doesn't. Things fall through the cracks or are pushed off of a desk and then replaced by the crime that happens next week. Plus cops have a short life span. They last twenty years at most and they get moved around from assignment to assignment and things just fall by the wayside and go unsolved. It's disappointing but true."

Whether it results in a conviction or not, every case begins with a police investigation. While patrol officers will usually be the first on the scene of a crime, it is the detectives that handle an investigation from start to finish. Detectives are part of a separate division in a police station and, depending on the size of the population and geographic area to be covered, may be broken out into specialized areas such as Organized Crime (narcotics, rackets, and so on), Major Offense (arson, burglary, homicide, sex crimes), or Technical Services (polygraph, forgery, photography, bombs). Most smaller departments have a generalized approach that takes advantage of limited staff levels and lower crime rates where detectives handle multiple tasks.

In either structure, the role of the detective is much the same. Detectives handle everything from the preliminary investigation and gathering of evidence to interviewing, interrogating, and eliminating suspects in the investigative phase. Contrary to popular belief and endless television movie reruns, a detective's job is not all adventure. In fact, most detectives will tell you that it's probably 90 percent paperwork and 10 percent running down leads. This may come as a surprise, but when you consider that they are responsible for investigating a crime from the minute it is assigned to them through its conclusion in court, the process of recording every detail can seem endless. This may be a bane for most detectives, but it can provide a wealth of material for the investigative writer.

"Secondary sources can vary in importance. I went through fifteen file drawers of records on the Texas murders, which helps build the overall story, but it doesn't make it come to life," notes Scott Anderson. "But what I found to be most helpful were the police reports on the case because you can see where they learn what and when. They really help you see the way the investigation unfolded and it helps create a timeline for the crime and how they solved it."

Every investigation begins with a police record of an offense, referred to as either a *reported crime* or a *known offense,* which leads to the pre-arrest investigation. Designed to gather information and evidence, this can involve interviewing witnesses and suspects, searching individuals and locations, and collecting evidence such as fingerprints, photos, bullet casings, tire- or footprints, or hair or clothing samples. Every detective's notes on a crime begin with several key facts: The time of notification, the time police arrived on the scene, the address and weather conditions, the identity of the victim and distinguishing characteristics (wounds, scars, tattoos, and so on), and photographs of the area. Other issues include noting the state of the victim's clothes (stains, rips, and so on), a street plan and diagrams of the house or apartment and yard, the position and condition of the body, and, if possible, an estimate of the time of death.

What is critical about this and any other information in an initial crime scene report is that it will reflect the circumstances before the area or evidence has been tampered with. As a rule, the police never open a crime scene unless all evidence has been gathered or secured for later analysis. In cases where there has been a murder or a sex crime, a Crime Scene Search Unit will often be dispatched to collect evidence. This can cover everything from making aerial photographs and measured sketches of the scene to sweeping the area with metal detectors and taking fingernail scrapings from a victim. When this evidence is gathered, it is usually forwarded to various departments such as the latent fingerprint unit, the scientific investigation unit, or the medical examiner for processing. One of the detective's roles in every murder investigation is to act as a liaison between all these forensic units within the department. Detectives also provide a direct link to the coroner's (or medical examiner's) office and the homicide bureau of the local prosecutor. All these offices maintain separate files on every murder, but the police can be circumspect about the information that goes in a file and you will have to compare the records carefully against information that will emerge later after the case is closed and people are more willing to talk.

"Police officers, by bitter experience, are very closed mouthed and very tight with files," says former policewoman Jay Fletcher. "They are careful about what they put on paper and then what they do with that paper. It has come back to haunt them too many times."

Even in cases of apparent suicide, most detectives treat an unnatural death as if it was a murder right from the start. But *murder* is a broad term, and the police have several standard classifications for it. At its most basic, *homicide* is a neutral term to describe the act of one human killing another without legal excuse; homicides are broadly classified as *justifiable, excusable,* or *felonious* to describe the conditions surrounding them. In turn, these are broken down into *first* and *second degrees* to indicate the seriousness of the act. While standards vary by state, first degree is used to indicate intent, premeditation, or killings that are part of a robbery or rape. Second degree routinely covers all other murders. Beyond these broad terms, there are a number of other designations designed to cover specific incidents. These include *vehicular homicide* (with a car), *accidental death* (circumstances that are not evil but seem suspicious), and *manslaughter* (killing without malice) which can be *voluntary* (as the result of a quarrel or in the heat of passion) or *involuntary* (in the course of performing a legal act in an illegal manner or without using due caution), among many others.

In most homicides, there are no witnesses. That means that police must use a variety of information sources and technical test procedures to gather evidence. Some of the key issues that are included in police records are the location and nature of the wounds, the origin and condition of the weapon, and the identity of the victims. Since police are trained not to rely on visual identifications of the deceased, they often look beyond the crime scene and into records such as fingerprints, dental charts, medical records that show the location of scars or broken bones, characteristics such as tattoos, identifying tags for allergies or medical conditions, or metal objects that may indicate ownership (lighters, knives, money clips, rings, and so on).

Investigating detectives sometimes estimate the time of death at the scene of the crime, but this is typically left to a pathologist from the coroner's office. Despite the fact that the method of murder might be obvious, the pathologist determines both the cause of death and the time at which death occurred as part of a thorough autopsy, and may also address the identity of the victim. Other items of interest may be found through the presence of drugs and alcohol in the bloodstream, evidence of sexual abuse, or the interval between the wounds and the time of death. Most detectives will attend the autopsy to provide additional background information or to recover evidence and will usually note details from this session in their reports.

Autopsies and death certificates are good sources for details and the coroner's office can be a helpful source of information in addition to anything found in a report. This is particularly true in smaller towns, where the position is frequently filled by a local undertaker. One item that often escapes examination is the qualifications of the coroner or pathologist performing the autopsy. In many cases, the position is an elective or appointive office, which does not always mean that the most qualified person is chosen for the post. The best medical examiners have been trained in forensic pathology, often with a specialty in areas such as toxicology, blood work, or dentistry, but many have not. It is essential to cross-check the coroner's findings with those of the police in the early stages of an investigation.

With the basics of the crime in hand, the detectives will turn to the issues of motives and suspects. Motives are not a legal necessity, but they are frequently the starting point for investigation. The other logical place to begin is the determination of who had the opportunity to commit the crime. In either case, one typically leads directly to another. That is, if someone had an opportunity to kill the victim, the detectives will examine whether or not there was a motive and vice versa. Witnesses (if any) are interviewed and then the circle widens to family members, friends, business associates, and other people who had any ongoing relationship with the deceased. Although every investigation is different, once a suspect has been determined a more intensive level of surveillance takes place to confirm or corroborate motive and to collect evidence. This stage can also provide additional material and documents including everything from search warrants and reports from interviews to requests for wiretaps.

Assembling evidence that is admissible in court is one of the primary roles of the detective. This means that information and supporting material must link the elements surrounding the crime directly to the suspect and that they must be gathered in a legal manner. To comply with this, search warrants validate the issue of probable cause. A search warrant is obtained after a detective files an affidavit with a judge outlining and substantiating the probable cause. This can include personal observations, physical evidence, hearsay from interviews, and a description of the place or places to be searched and what evidence the searchers will be looking for to further the investigation. If granted, the warrant will specify a period of validity and a specified time when the search can take place (usually only during daylight hours). The language of both the affidavit and the warrant are extremely specific and provide another excellent source of details.

If a suspect has been targeted and specific facts emerge providing links to the crime, the police may detain and question the suspect without formal arrest or charge if they believe that they have probable cause. Probable cause is not a guess or a gut feeling; it has to be supported by specific facts and reasonable conclusions drawn from the investigation. While laws vary by state, the extent of this temporary detention can go as far as taking the suspect's fingerprints, but rarely allows the police to take someone to the police station for questioning. The police may legally call and invite the suspect to come in and talk or may briefly stop someone and ask a few questions, but to bring people into the station they will have to be formally arrested. That means that the police will have to have an arrest warrant, obtained in much the same way that a search warrant is, that is very specific in terms of the charges and the identifying characteristics of the suspect.

When an arrest takes place and after the suspect is informed of the Miranda rights, the police may seize items found "in plain view" around the suspect if they believe them to be related to the crime. All evidence is entered into a report and maintained in an evidence room at the station. At this point, the police need no warrant to make the suspect undergo fingerprinting and photography, provide hair and blood samples, undergo breath testing, and remove objects hidden in body cavities. Other things the police can do include making the suspect stand in a lineup, speak so possible witnesses can hear and identify the voice, and strip for inspection of any scars or identifying characteristics. Suspects will also be subjected to interrogation about the crime and their relationship to it, a process that might or might not lead to a confession of guilt.

Due to the complexity of evidentiary rules, all of these stages will be carefully reported on and will be contained in a variety of police records on the case. But when looking at these records, it is important not to take them at face value. Writers should examine the thoroughness of the reports and how well the police preserved the crime scene through sketches, photographs, and notes as well as how they collected and preserved the evidence that allowed them to reconstruct the crime. It is also important to look at all possible motives and suspects that the police have—or haven't—contacted, because these are issues that will have to be reviewed as part of the research process to provide the most complete picture possible in recreating the events leading up to the crime.

Unfortunately, many police officers have come to take a dim view of journalists and can be reticent or outright hostile when asked for information unless they know the writer's opinions to be openly pro-police. This can come into play when trying to secure access to police records, which can be more difficult to obtain than one might think because there is no uniform approach to filing them. Some might be listed by complaint, which means you have to know who filed it, or by the time of day and date. If you only have the name of the suspect, you might be in for a lot of searching.

As a longtime police reporter, Edna Buchanan eventually came to be accepted by the police she covered and had many avenues for information. But she is also quick to point out that "sometimes cops want to tell you everything, sometimes not. But some are really ornery and don't like the press and I would have to work my way around them."

Attitudes notwithstanding, one of the keys to this riddle for the uninitiated can be to develop a relationship with the department's Public Information Officer. These people can help locate and explain reports, as well as access other documents and databases the department might maintain. Another approach is to review a police department organization manual, which will outline how and where reports are to be filed. Search warrants are available through local courthouses and can be accessed fairly easily. In stations where cases are filed chronologically, a review of the daily booking information can be a great place to start because it will have the basic but essential facts about a case—suspect's identifying characteristics, charges, name of arresting officers and agency, and so forth—which can provide additional places to start looking.

The Judicial System

Following an arrest, the suspect is booked, subjected to a criminal records check and a session to obtain information such as fingerprints and samples, and then held in custody in a holding cell. During this time the police will interrogate the suspect and this process may be taped, videotaped, or recorded by a stenographer to ensure admissibility. The police will also have turned over their evidence to the prosecutor, who will have to make a decision on whether or not to file an indictment that formally charges the suspect with the crime and asks the court to bring the case forward to trial. Depending on the state in which the suspect was arrested, the next step will be either a preliminary hearing (or arraignment) or an appearance before a grand jury.

In about half the United States, a state will require that the prosecutors and police make their case in front of a grand jury. Selected from voter registration lists or driver's license databases (or some similar listing), these juries meet in closed sessions (the public, including reporters, is not allowed) where the presentations are one-sided. Given the format, prosecutors generally prefer grand juries. But there are ways to get information from a grand jury. In some states, such as California, the transcripts of the jury's proceedings are not sealed after an indictment has been issued and can be had just by asking the judge for them. In other cases, the subpoenas issued for witnesses to appear before the grand jury are part of the public record and can be found at the courthouse, as can the names of any witnesses who were reimbursed for expenses. A careful examination of the court's voucher records will produce many witnesses' names and addresses, thus providing leads to possible interviews.

The alternative is a preliminary hearing (or probable cause hearing) before a judge in open court, where the prosecution will have to share its information (known as *discovery*) with the defense. This is the exact opposite of the grand jury approach and can provide a wealth of information, much of which may never make it into the trial. Transcripts of these proceedings can be obtained through the court. With the evidence from the state's case laid out before them in court, defense counsel may move to have certain pieces dismissed or the charges dropped.

These motions lead to a pretrial hearing, an event that many writers tend to overlook as a footnote to the overall case. While these hearings may serve as a platform for all sorts of allegations against the police and the state's case, some of the complaints are quite real and revealing. This is particularly true in the area of how the police interrogated the suspect or obtained a confession. An adroit defender can elicit background information about the police officers attached to the case—information that can be quite revealing for a writer—as well as their investigative techniques and rationale. Other pretrial hearings can focus on lie detector tests, dismissal of charges, change of venue, the composition of the jury, bail money, or the capability of the defendant to stand trial.

With these details resolved, the case is assigned to a judge. Again, this varies by state, with some using a first-come-first-assigned basis or a lottery system of picking cases. Despite their claim to impartiality, judges are human like everyone else and have their own biases when it comes to both individual prosecutors and either the police or the issue of defendants' rights. Opinions can be gathered by asking around about any judges' reputations, but a more thorough approach is to cross-check such opinions against a review of the judges' decisions in previous cases to see if the claims can be corroborated.

Outside of the events that constitute a progression toward a trial, a steady stream of paperwork from all related parties and agencies effectively mirrors the workings of the justice system. This includes everything from letters, filings, and police reports to search warrants, depositions, and autopsy reports. The majority of these documents will reside in what is known as the *court file* on the case. This is kept by the court clerk at the courthouse where the case will be heard and is considered to be part of the public record. You can get the file from the clerk by giving the name of the defendant or the date of the offense or the case number, but you cannot take it out of the building or room that is provided for reading it. You can usually copy part or all of it, and you can always take notes on the more interesting sections. Naturally, this is a file that will continue to grow until the case is resolved and it can provide an enormous level of detail and leads to potentially useful material.

The depositions of witnesses (or potential witnesses) often proves to be one of the richest sources in the court file. These are highly focused interviews taken in the presence of the prosecutor and the defense attorney, both of whom will ask questions, and the witness's own lawyer and a court stenographer. While dedicated to the details of the case, a deposition can also contain revealing personal information. A wealth of background material often can be derived from the depositions of those witnesses who are never called to the stand. Although highly repetitive, occasionally technically dense (in the case of medical or expert witnesses), and frequently boring to read, depositions are useful because they are taken closer to the date of the actual crime than in-court testimony or after-the-decision interviews, and they are exploratory in nature. That means that memories are fresher and facts may surface that might be inadmissible in court, but could prove valuable in charting a narrative.

Once the pretrial motions have been heard, waived, or dismissed, the case will proceed to trial unless a plea bargain can be arranged. Plea bargains allow the defendant to plead guilty as charged, but often to a lesser offense or for a promise from the prosecutor to request a more lenient sentence. If the defendant won't plead guilty, the case goes to trial before a judge or jury or, in the majority of murder cases, both. The trial involves the judge, jury, defendant and defense lawyer, the prosecuting attorney or team, witnesses, court officials, and all evidence related to the case.

For all intents and purposes, the typical criminal trial consists of nine basic stages. These include:

- *Opening statements:* An opening statement by the prosecution outlining their case and how they intend to prove the defendant's guilt, and a similar statement by the defense, focusing on the defendant's innocence.

- *Presentation of evidence:* The presentation of evidence by the prosecution. Evidence is either *direct* or *circumstantial.* Direct evidence is witness testimony, primary documents, photographs, fingerprints, or weapons. Circumstantial evidence is a series of facts that establish a route to a logical conclusion without the presence of direct evidence.

- *Witness testimony:* The presentation of witnesses in a logical manner on the witness stand. The prosecutor asks non-leading questions in what is known as direct examination to present the case. Then the defense attorney is allowed to cross-examine the witness regarding the testimony and any questions that the prosecutor may not have asked. Cross-examination is an option that does not have to be employed.

○ *Resting the case:* Using the legal principles that define the rules of evidence, the prosecution will present their entire case until they feel they have met the burden of proof necessary to convict. Then the prosecution will rest the case.

○ *Presentation of the defense:* The roles are reversed as the defense presents its case through the direct examination of its own witnesses, whom the prosecution can then cross-examine.

○ *Rebuttal:* Once the defense rests, the prosecution has the chance to offer evidence in rebuttal to the defense's case. This can be followed by a similar move on the defense's part and can continue with each side taking turns for as long as the judge permits. These exchanges must cover only material previously presented, and may be further restricted by the presiding judge.

○ *Final arguments:* While most defense attorneys usually move to dismiss the charges at this point outside the presence of the jury, the prosecution will oppose dismissal and then the judge will rule on the motion. Then the prosecution will re-present their case, stressing the highlights and strengths in a way that they believe will be most persuasive. The defense will follow in the same manner.

- *Verdict:* Following receipt of the judge's instructions on how to focus their understanding of the evidence, the jury will retire to debate the evidence in private. They will reach a decision and deliver it to the court.
- *Sentence:* With the trial complete, the witnesses and jury are dismissed. If found guilty, the defendant will be sentenced by the judge. At this point, the transcripts of the trial and all evidence introduced during it are entered into the public record.

While the events of the trial might figure prominently in the final story, there is an ongoing debate among true crime writers over the value of attending it. Some think that it is largely a waste of time and money, while others think that it improves both their overall sense of the story and their long-term access to the people involved in it.

"I sometimes cover a case while it's going on and I think it makes a difference in terms of being a better story because you've got everyone in one place at the same time so you've got the dynamic of the trial and people's personalities come out under that stress," says Fred Rosen. "It's quite revealing, plus you get to see the wheels of justice turning. But it's tougher to do from a cost basis for the writer because it takes more time and costs more money and you've got to look at the advance on the project."

After the Trial

There is also an alternative to covering a trial. Every word uttered in court is recorded by an official stenographer working on a specialized machine. This material will later be transcribed into a comprehensive transcript but, depending on the length and complexity of the trial, it may be some time before it is accessible. Rules concerning transcripts vary widely, but they are always part of the court's approach in cases where the death penalty is involved. Transcripts are indexed by volume and, like the court file, the transcript becomes part of the public record and is a helpful source when it comes to reviewing liability issues later on.

"The transcript is a starting point that gives you a cast of characters and a list of who you will need to talk to," says Lowell Cauffiel. "It's also a big part of your legal protection, because anything that's said on the stand is fair game and it establishes the parameters of what you can write about without fear of lawsuits. But transcripts aren't always completely accurate and I check everything from the brand names of things to weather reports to the time and place of events."

Other writers argue that the tedium and expense of a transcript is a waste since much of the material is devoted to legal maneuvering or simply repeats what can be found in a deposition. Some writers will manage to borrow the transcript from one of the attorneys involved in the case and copy it for future reference while focusing on other material.

"In my opinion, the trial transcript is the least important thing in all the research you might do," says Jack Olsen. "The stuff that's interesting to me usually isn't admissible in court because it's the background material that gives you the story. I'm bored by transcripts, but they are good for sources you might have missed and you can't be sued for anything in them and that's important."

Another issue that will often surface in court will be the introduction of crime scene photographs to the record. As a rule, true crime publishers have always employed photographs from a case as a means of adding to the authenticity of the story and separating the book from the hundreds of others on the market offering the vicarious excitement of a mystery or a thriller. Readers of true crime are known to consider photographs important, often glancing at the cover copy and proceeding directly to the photo spread to determine their interest in buying the book.

"Photos are important in true crime because it sets the genre apart," explains Charles Spicer of St. Martin's. "This is particularly important in the paperback market where the bottom line on photos is 'gross is great.'"

Local newspapers usually have photos in their files as part of the existing coverage of the case, but the selection of published pictures tends to exclude things unsuitable for a family audience. In cases that attract a lot of attention, many of these papers have come to see the photographs as a profit center and will charge steep fees for them, so a writer has to have several sources in mind.

"The best crime scene photos come from the police department but it depends on the state," says Lowell Cauffiel. "For example, Florida has a wide open Freedom of Information Act that lets you have everything, even family photos. If there's a real good shot in the newspaper, I'll order one but they can be expensive—as much as $50 to $100 apiece. Some small papers will give them away for free, but everyone has seen them and you want to have something fresh to set the book apart. But sometimes you can get a photographer who has shot personal film on the side or there's wire shooters who retain the rights to their own negatives and you can buy the shots from them."

But as important as photographs are, some publishers consider them to be an issue of market dynamics rather than essential to the validity of a book. "Unlike other editors, I don't use gory photos in our inserts. The worst might be a body in a body bag being carried out because, at their heart, true crime stories are human interest stories," says Putnam/Penguin's Michaela Hamilton. "As a result, I tend to use people and place photos to capture the characters and the setting. If you look at *Fatal Vision* you will see that it was released as a hard cover with no photos because it was aimed at an upper-class audience and it was felt that it wouldn't enhance the appeal. But we added a photo insert when we did the paperback reprint because we thought that end of the market would respond to it."

While essential to fleshing out the pivotal facts of a story and turning it into a compelling narrative, much of this research is a precursor to the primary source of information that a writer relies on—the personal interview.

Chapter Four

FACE TO FACE

Interviewing Sources

Secondary sources are essential in developing a comprehensive background of revealing detail against which the narrative of a story can be set. They provide the depth and color necessary to show the forces and motives that have shaped a character's behavior in relation to a crime. But few things are as revealing as a combination of dialogue and personal admission when it comes to advancing a plot, exposing a long-hidden secret, assigning culpability, or admitting guilt. That's what makes both a character and a story come to life and the only way to get that material is through the personal interview.

As the core of every research effort, interviews with primary sources come in many forms. For the most part, these are not "interviews" in the traditional notion of a one-on-one, question-and-answer format. In fact, such a formal, journalistic approach is often the death knell when it comes to extracting sensitive material because it can make people feel confronted rather than coaxed. Their response often will be a tendency to withhold information rather than divulge it, especially in cases where a murder has occurred. Shame, sorrow, anger, and guilt are just a few of the more powerful emotions that dominate the ways in which people express themselves after the fact and many involved in a case will be reluctant to talk openly or directly. In light of this, most people are usually not interested in taking part in any process that is remotely confrontational, especially with a stranger.

"You don't know what you don't know, so how do you deal with that? My way is to just be there and see what happens," Harry MacLean says about his approach to interviewing reluctant subjects. "A lot of the big breaks I got happened just because of that. But you have to have a good intuitive sense about dealing with people. You have to figure out where they're coming from and be empathetic. So you talk about crops, coon dogs, their kids, whatever. A lot of time you only have thirty seconds to get across and connect with them, but you have to be there for those situations to occur. You cannot go in with a list of questions. You have to let things evolve. That's what kills journalists who try these books. You have to have a relationship and go back four, five, six times before someone will talk to you; it can't be fifteen questions and out the door. You have to let them go where they want in a conversation."

This is where the secondary research comes in. Although it will eventually play a prominent role in helping to recreate a richly detailed atmosphere once the writing begins, it is also central in helping to determine "who" you have to talk to and "what" information you need to get from them. The "who" may come from the trial transcript, a quote in a newspaper article or a broadcast transcript, a name on a contract, or a lead from a local reporter who has been covering the case. But regardless of how you identify potential contacts, you need to know as much as possible about their relationship to the crime and the people involved to know "what" you're looking for from an interview with them. Secondary research can provide that critical background information, but the depth and quality of material an interview can yield will vary widely. Some sessions will provide a simple confirmation of something you already know to be true; others will reveal something you only suspected or send you off on an entirely new set of leads. That means an interview can be as simple as a chat in a car or a bar, a phone call to follow up on something, or a comprehensive conversation about a case. A new fact, revelation, or missing detail may come the second, third, or seventh time you talk to someone, but it almost always adds a firsthand level of information that you already have in hand—a level that no successful story can be without. The trick is in getting people to talk.

"I get cooperation by hanging around, that's the school of interviewing I came from," says Jack Olsen, whose interview tapes are used as instructional material in courses at the University of Oregon. "I'm a hanger, I don't quiz people, I sit down and have a conversation with them. You've got to develop a spark of empathy with the person or you're dead. Sometimes I go back four or five times before I'll get something good. You can't just sit down and give someone the third degree to get them to tell you something, but everyone's got a story to tell and they want to tell it. So if you're sympathetic, they will eventually tell you. But it takes time."

Access to Sources

This is one of the reasons why true crime can take so long to write. Not only does the process of establishing relationships take time, but the course of running down every lead can frequently run interview lists up over the hundred-person mark. This figure can easily double if the case is complex or spread across several states. For the most part, interview subjects can be divided into three basic areas based on their direct relationship to the case: the police, the victim's family, the criminal, and the defense attorneys. These are primary interviews and they are essential, but there are also secondary sources that can be extremely helpful. These can include friends, neighbors, former spouses and lovers, co-workers, club or church members, and professional contacts such as lawyers or doctors. Although many of these people may be reluctant to talk, a writer should never assume that they won't grant an interview. People often will divulge things for reasons that are not readily apparent or even share information while simultaneously refusing to be interviewed. Of course, some individuals will go out of their way to paint a positive picture of either the subject or themselves in the face of a grim scenario, but that is just human nature. Besides, hearing about someone's good qualities will help capture a more comprehensive picture of a character's personality. But the key is to get someone close to the case to start talking to you. Once that's done, you can always cite information or a reference from that interview in approaching other sources because many people will be reticent to speak unless they know that one of the primary players is cooperating on a story.

"I didn't have a direct source on my first book and I struggled with every piece of information in it. Now I won't do a book unless I have a solid source, either the criminal, or a cop, or a family member," says Jay Fletcher. "I've sniffed after many stories that didn't fly, because you have to look at a lot of them. Since I'm a former cop, I usually start with the detective and then have them get in touch with the family and make an introduction."

When a personal introduction isn't available, the best route to a source is usually the most direct one. This can be either a letter or a phone call, but most writers prefer to write a letter when they have to make their own connections. Why? Because a phone call can be screened or avoided, or it may come at an inconvenient time for the source—someone you are ideally trying to develop some sort of relationship with. There can also be misunderstandings in a conversation that can come back to haunt a writer when it comes time to corroborate a source's willingness to talk. Letters solve this problem by allowing the source to see where the writer is coming from, what the story will be about, and what kind of general information will be on the table. Reading allows sources to consider the request in an unhurried fashion and makes any decision they make to cooperate their own. This approach is a prerequisite when contacting a criminal in jail.

While effective, using a letter to request an interview comes with several caveats. The first is to be as consistent as possible when writing such letters to multiple sources. People involved in a significant or unusual crime tend to be tied together in ways that are not readily apparent and you should assume that they will be talking to each other. If there are gross inconsistencies in your approach, people who compare notes will doubt your trustworthiness—

and they will compare notes. It is usually helpful to cite your professional credentials as a means of separating you from other people who have been requesting interviews and to emphasize the fact that you are working on a book. For some reason, books are taken more seriously than articles and "authors" have more credibility than "reporters." Finally, it is helpful to be as general as possible when mentioning the kind of information you are seeking and to avoid any direct mention of an interview. In most cases, a passing reference to your desire to "run down some leads," "fill in some gaps," or simply "check some facts" will do the job.

"You can't appear to be too interested at first and you have to be patient," Lowell Cauffiel says. "I always make people feel that I am like them, rather than different from them. I will use old newspaper tricks like send flowers to people who turn me down and thank them. I never tell anyone that I want to interview them because that allows them to turn you down before they meet you. I just say that I want to come over and introduce myself and explain what I am doing. That I'm doing this book and you'll be in it and I'd like to tell you about it, whether or not you want to be involved is up to you. I always set a meeting in a neutral place and never bring a tape or a notebook. Instead, I give them a published book, tell them about my philosophy, and tell them what I'm going to do and then say I think it would be helpful to participate. That gets 80 percent of the people involved on board."

If sources do not respond to a letter or there is a time constraint on either their part or yours (say, they're leaving town; you've got a deadline), a phone call is not only appropriate, it is often the only way. If a letter has been sent, you can say that you are simply following up on it, that you are aware that they are busy but you just need a small amount of time. Be polite. If the source seems harried, ask if there is a better time for you to call back. If someone continues to dodge you or seems reluctant, you may want to try to assuage any fears they might have by using an intermediary—someone whom you have already interviewed who you know to be friendly with them—to contact them and vouch for you. The goal is to get your source sitting across from you, willing to listen to your case, and answering your questions.

But some people will choose not to talk. At least at first. As always, the key is consistency and perseverance and if subjects decline, then don't hesitate to give them some time to reflect before trying again. A classic technique is to play a waiting game and try to back someone into an interview by talking to everyone around them. At that point, they can be given the option of going on record with their own version of events, sometimes with the guarantee of a pseudonym, or simply having to read about everybody else's opinion of what happened and their role in it without having the chance to defend themselves, their actions, or their point of view. In many instances, they will come to that conclusion on their own. The trick is to state your case, be patient, and not to shut the door to them.

"Interviews can vary," Edna Buchanan explains. "Survivors' families often want to talk with you as a means of catharsis, while others stay away and want to forget it. But if I had the door slammed in my face or someone hung up on me, I'd give it a minute and call or knock again. Just to give them a minute to reflect on their decision and half of the time they'd talk. Even if I left without an interview, I'd always leave my card and scribble a note saying 'If you ever want to talk. . . .' Sometimes it takes weeks before they're ready to talk and if they can't get in touch with you, you'll miss a key opportunity that can make the difference in a major story."

Sometimes a source will approach a writer offering information without ever having been asked to do so. This is not completely out of the ordinary, but it should be viewed with some caution. In many cases, people will have a personal agenda to advance and, when there is a clear bias to their comments, all information should be double-checked for accuracy. Other times, people will want money or, if they perceive the information as crucial, a percentage of the writer's advance or profits. The current practice among some tabloids to pay sources and the recent spate of high-profile cases that have produced bestselling books have combined to heighten the public's awareness of what information can be worth. But paying for information is not considered to be an ethical practice among investigative writers or mainstream jour-nalists and most writers have an innate distrust of any "facts" that have been exchanged for money.

Some Basic Rules

Like each source, each interview will be different. Some people will want to tell you everything, others almost nothing, and then there are those who consider them-selves crafty enough to assume that they will be the one getting information out of you. Whenever possible, it is essential to try and identify with the source's background and experience in a neutral way that seems empathetic. The idea is to start building a rapport that will foster the atmosphere of trust necessary to get someone to drop their guard. Prior research should have provided a few clues regarding areas of interest—sports, neighborhood or civic activities, a group they belong to—to use as material for an ice-breaker to get the conversation going. Since most people love to talk about themselves, try to steer the initial conversation in that direction; don't start by talking about the case.

"I'll use a tape recorder or take notes, but at first I'll often have nothing and will tell people, say, that I'm interested in the area and the lifestyle," Harry MacLean says. "I'll ask all sorts of general questions like 'What do you do on Sunday afternoon? What's the school like?'— really innocuous stuff, just to get a feel for the area. I'm always slow to pull that notebook out and when I do I'll often say 'Well, I have a bad memory, do you mind if I take a few notes?' People are lonely and love to talk, love to tell their story. I really don't say much. I just keep them going with things like 'Really? That right? How's that work?'"

When in doubt, be slightly more formal than you think necessary. This can often be as simple as adhering to the basics of good manners: Calling the source Mr. or Mrs., not smoking or chewing gum, not touching anyone on the arm, and not being overly familiar in general. Small talk and opening pleasantries are important in creating an atmosphere of comfort and trust. To foster this, you should appear relaxed and pleasant and dress in a way that subtly reinforces a sense of commonality. While there are no rules for this, common sense dictates that interviews with professionals such as lawyers and police require basic business attire while jeans would be appropriate for an interview in a working-class bar. When in doubt, always focus on what would make you blend in rather than stand out.

"On my first book, there was a reporter from *Playboy* who came to town and treated everyone like yokels," MacLean adds. "He dressed in a new pair of jeans and had a bottle of Jack Daniels hanging out of his rear pocket because that's what he thought rednecks did. Well, they don't and they gave him a huge amount of misinformation and ran him around. You can't underestimate the people you're interviewing."

To reduce any potential anxiety about an initial interview, it is often advisable to let sources pick the location where you will meet. This allows them some sense of control while subtly increasing their overall comfort level. In most cases, this is a public place because people will feel more relaxed in a social setting or just safer talking to a stranger when there are others around.

"I prefer to interview people in restaurants, bars, or in their houses because that's where they are most comfortable," Darcy O'Brien says of his approach to interviewing. "It's also great to see their own houses because the symbolism of their own lives is in there and that's really valuable to a writer. That's something that a lot of nonfiction writers miss, the fact that everything's symbolic, even someone's ties, even what's *not* in their house. There's a story behind all of these things and it can help you discover more about their personalities and their lives."

Once the interview begins, be sure to notice any signs of discomfort in the source's body language. This can be everything from nail biting to crossed arms and legs and is completely normal behavior. The key is to remain calm, use humor, and maintain eye contact while acting as if this is just another routine conversation. Don't jump right into a list of questions that may come off as being confrontational. In most cases, simply chatting and listening without offering any judgments will go a long way toward building rapport and getting the interview headed in the right direction.

Once you do get people talking, it is important to have a structure to your line of questioning. This does not mean that you have to have a list that you refer to constantly, but there should be a logical flow to the issues you want to cover. Questions should be direct, but leading questions along the lines of "You really did kill her, didn't you?" usually draw a sharp response and can end the session and preclude any further opportunities to talk. Be patient and listen to whatever you are being told. The goal is to keep the conversation going in a way that will allow you to return for more information at a later date if you need to. Sources will wander, but that isn't necessarily a bad sign. In fact, it is often an indicator that someone is feeling more comfortable. But a list of questions and topics to cover will help you reframe the session to advance the flow of material.

One of the central issues that is widely misunderstood by both writers and sources is what the phrase "off the record" actually means. Many sources feel that if they preface a remark with such a disclaimer, it will never make its way into a story. But the writer should set the ground rules once the subject is broached. In most instances, the information can be considered to be background material to a story that can be confirmed elsewhere. In others, it pays to ask if the statement can be used "without attribution"—as fact but not as a direct quote—or if you can paraphrase the comments to retain the meaning while deflecting attribution. This can often be helpful when reconstructing dialogue, especially if it can be confirmed elsewhere. If there is any doubt, it is always better to ask "Can I quote you?" or discuss issues of attribution to clear up any potential misunderstandings before they occur. Be specific about how you intend to use the information.

As the interview unfolds, try to elicit emotion as well as information. Ask people how they feel or felt about another person or an event. Keep the conversation rolling with small affirmations or questions, avoid gaps of silence, and remain focused on where you want the interview to go. Always leave the door open to follow-up sessions or the chance to check a fact and inquire if there is anybody else the source thinks you should talk to about the case.

Notes Versus Tapes

A common issue of debate among writers is whether it is better to take notes or tape record an interview. In either case, people can tense up when they realize that what they are saying is going on the record. But the writer must make a decision about how to record conversations for both literary and legal reasons. Some writers will do both, but that can be distracting for both the source and the writer and the interview will suffer as a result.

Many writers who rely on notes do so more out of a dislike of tape recorders than a preference for a pad and pen. Tape recorders can break, the batteries can run out, or the tape can end and the writer can forget to flip it. This can be a distraction for the writer who will constantly worry about whether everything is working rather than concentrate on the interview. But note taking is an art unto itself, and it takes practice to be able to keep a conversation moving while managing to simultaneously record it. Many experienced journalists either learn shorthand or devise their own form of it to keep things going.

It is a matter of fact that, even with shorthand, most people cannot write as fast as someone else can talk. This means that most writers will have to paraphrase sections of the conversation while still managing to get a few solid quotes verbatim. When a source jumps ahead to another important comment, don't hesitate—go with the jump and then try to circle back to the original quote to flesh it out. Never hesitate to ask someone to repeat a specific quote to ensure accuracy. Unfortunately, people rarely say the same thing in the same way twice and that may muddy the meaning of the original statement or open it to debate. Whenever possible, try to sit down immediately after a session to record your notes with any accompanying observations about the source or the setting, including the time, date, and names of individuals present at the interview.

"When I interview people, I take notes rather than use a tape recorder for the same reason the FBI takes notes," Darcy O'Brien says. "A tape recorder tends to intimidate the subject or it encourages them to put on an act and become false. Also it can break and cause problems and I worry about that."

The downside of note taking is that it is not uncommon for subjects to claim that they were misquoted after the fact. This is the reason most writers—and every publisher's legal department—prefer tapes. Taping conversations ensures total accuracy, establishes a definitive record of what was said, and allows interviewers to ask more questions in a short amount of time than they would be able to raise if they were taking notes. Tapes enable the interviewer to concentrate on the nuances of the conversation and coax as much information out of a subject as possible, and also provide a definitive source on any possibly controversial material that may be disclosed. Some writers swear by them while others swear at them, and some split the difference in the name of getting the story however they can.

"I usually use tapes and am always amazed at how many people will let you do that," says Ann Rule. "But on a recent case in Kansas City I couldn't go in as a media visitor because they don't want to make the prisoners famous. As a regular visitor you can't bring in any writing materials, so I went out to the car and immediately taped my recollections of the conversation. I prefer to use tape because I like to have absolutely accurate quotes, but I often take notes as well."

Since many people can become nervous around a tape recorder, most writers will begin an interview in a conversational tone and then produce a tape recorder. This is often done under the guise of "Well, I have a lousy memory . . ." or a simple "Do you mind . . . ?" while setting the recorder off to the side. Although they come in all shapes and sizes, the most popular units seem to be high-quality, voice-activated microcassette recorders that are reliable yet unobtrusive. Larger models with separate microphones work extremely well, but are usually better suited to a situation where reproduction quality is an issue, such as a broadcast environment. This is because they take some practice in setting up, a process that tends to distract a source in all but the most formal interview situations.

For phone interviews, tape recording is essential in getting a conversation down accurately. This can be done with a small adapter available from any local electronics or audio dealer. However, it is essential to let the source know that you are recording the conversation in the event of any post-publication legal action. Should a source balk at the possibility of being recorded, the most tactful way out of any disagreement is to state that you are taping only as a means of guaranteeing absolute accuracy.

Interviewing the Police

Of all the people to be interviewed for a true crime story, the only group that will uniformly balk at the sight of a tape recorder will be the police. The aggressive nature of the modern media, coupled with internal legacies and myths about cops whose words have come back to haunt them and ruin a case, has made most police officers highly reticent about discussing a crime or placing even the slightest bias in the records they assemble regarding it. The issues of legal admissibility and attribution in the press are foremost in every cop's mind when it comes to setting facts down on paper or going on the record in an interview. While they are keenly aware of the leeway a notepad offers in terms of deniability, they are equally conscious of the absolute credibility of their own voice on a tape. That's why even a highly skilled interviewer with a microphone will get only monosyllabic answers to the most innocuous questions. This is problematic because police cooperation is often essential when tracking down a story. Still, the creative researcher always finds a way to get to one of the most important sources.

"I've always had great luck with cops, district attorneys, and defense lawyers. You have to convince them that you're not hooking up with one side or another," Harry MacLean explains. "I drink all the time with cops because that's where you get the information. There's always a cop bar and I hang out in it. Sometimes the case would never come up, and then one day it will. I always take notes with cops because they're comfortable with that and they can deny it later. They hate tape recorders. But they're great characters and are often accessible after they see you around for a while. A lot of them see themselves as a character in a book, so if you say that you want to portray them as they are, they'll cooperate with you. A lot of time they do the heavy lifting and then the lawyers or the politicians will take credit."

Police cooperation can come in many forms. Once you have earned their trust, often through sheer persistence or a reference from a mutually trusted source, they can be extremely helpful in providing new leads or background material. They will open up record rooms, provide addresses or phone numbers, or introduce you to other players involved in the case. But the police, especially detectives, are often in a difficult position. Pressured by their own leaders, the political structure, and the press to solve a crime quickly, they are vilified if it takes too long or if mistakes are made. Caught between the representatives of the public they work for and the world of the criminals they pursue, they often feel alone and at odds with everyone but themselves. That's why an introduction from another officer or the ability to produce a published book that shows the police in a favorable light goes a long way in terms of identifying a writer as a "friend of law enforcement" when it comes to getting help. Another aid is having a good attitude and the ability to convey a sense of understanding about the position they are in, particularly on a high-profile case.

"The way to a cop's heart is a good joke and a light-hearted attitude," says Lowell Cauffiel. "They spend their whole days dealing with bottom feeders so when they are off the job they tend to be very funny, cynical people. They are hilarious, that's how they get through their days, and that's how you get to them. Most cops want to get recognition for their work and most of the people who work on a case, who solve it, don't get recognition. So when someone comes along and wants to play up their career case they'll go for it."

Interviewing the Victim's Family

While the police may be difficult due to a wariness of the press as a result of previous experience, the victim's family can be a challenge because they typically have no experience. This is not to say that people are unsophisticated or unwilling, but they are often reticent because they are overwhelmed by grief and anger and they quickly find themselves deluged by reporters asking questions or making allegations. Modern press coverage can be relentless and few lives can bear up to a level of scrutiny that focuses on turning up every piece of the past as a means of getting a "scoop." This makes many families wary, distrustful, and inaccessible until well after a case has been resolved. Even then, it can be difficult to get access unless there is someone willing to vouch for you.

"I always start with the detective and let them take their time," explains Jay Fletcher. "We chat about this or that and they will start with talking about the crime endlessly because they, along with everybody else, think that's what the book is all about. But I know that it's really about everything else surrounding it and, besides, I already know about the crime. After they get done with all that, I say 'Okay, now tell me about the family.' In every case, they say, 'The family loves me.' That's because he's the only guy who looks like he's trying to give them some sort of satisfaction, who will sit in their living room and say, 'Look, I hate this bastard as much as you do.' From a practical basis, having the detective hold your hand and introduce you, they will open their home to you."

But many writers find that coming to a case after the fact has a distinct advantage that few reporters can match. After the court case has been closed and a criminal convicted, the family is left alone with its grief and sense of emptiness and the belief that everyone has forgotten the terrible tragedy that has befallen them. The appearance of a writer who wants to know the whole story and to write a book that brings their loved one back to life on the page is often more than a family can resist. But a writer can't abuse that trust. If the victim had less than a savory past, you must clear up any related issues surrounding the truth up front or else recriminations (and lawsuits) are sure to follow.

Some families will try to exchange their story for a percentage of the rights to a book or movie. Most writers will never offer any percentage of ownership to a book, but will often consider the issue of film rights. The standard practice for this is to offer a share of the fee if an option on the book is picked up and the film goes into production. This enables writers to get total access to the story, retain rights to their own work, and yet see that the family profits if the book moves to another medium where they can build that fee into their overall agreement. But sometimes there are unusual circumstances that warrant another course.

"I usually pick fairly remote cases that hardly anyone else knew about and the point is to make them interesting and not to capitalize on the publicity that was already there," Darcy O'Brien says of his subjects. "But in one of my books I had to sign over a percentage of my royalties to get the exclusive rights of the victim's family. It was a difficult choice, but it made me feel better because it would have been exploitive to make them go through revealing all of that pain without some sort of compensation. That's unusual and I haven't done it again."

Interviewing the Criminal

Getting the criminal's side of the story presents an entirely different range of problems. The first is that convicted criminals are shielded by the court and penal systems, neither of which has any interest in giving them any more publicity or notoriety than they already have earned. Court-appointed lawyers who have lost their cases can be notoriously uncooperative and a writer can find access a problem. Appointments can be difficult to get, even harder to justify, and then subject to ground rules that make information difficult to get.

Most writers approach criminals either directly or through their lawyers via a letter requesting an interview. Some writers who have covered a case through the courts will attempt to use their presence to develop a level of familiarity that they can leverage later on or will even go so far as to slip the criminal a note in court requesting an opportunity to talk. While approaches vary, one of the most effective is to promise that you will put all of your efforts into running down any leads that may exonerate the criminal. This often plays to people's belief that they are in charge and you are, in effect, working for them as an unpaid private investigator. Of course, if the criminal is convicted, there's probably very little information that has been missed by the investigators and you haven't promised anything that you can't deliver.

"I write a letter to the criminal—not their lawyer—because I want this guy to talk to me based on his decision alone," Jay Fletcher says of her approach. "I am very careful when I write to him that I am not offering any promises, no cajoling, no seducing. Just a very short, clear letter that says I am writing a book about the murder of 'whomever' for which you have been convicted. If you want to say anything about this crime that reflects your point of view or any facts, I will represent it accurately in this book. That's it. I'm not giving anything up when I make that promise because readers don't care what the perpetrator feels."

Once you have gained access, dealing with the criminal is similar to dealing with any other source interviewed for the story. The only catch is that these people are superb manipulators who think they can beat the system despite all the evidence to the contrary. That's where you may have to go against your own natural sensibilities or put judgments on hold. To get information out of killers, you have to appear as if you are on their side and to do that means that you must manipulate the manipulator without losing sight of yourself or your goals for the story.

"There's an old cop saying that applies to dealing with criminals: 'Treat a whore like a lady and a lady like a whore,'" Lowell Cauffiel says. "I treat criminals with utmost respect, am very friendly with them, and always make them feel that they are in control of the situation. The typical psycho is a manipulator and if they feel that they can do that to you you'll get in. Most good journalists seem to have a lot of apparent flaws, they tend to be somewhat odd people, and people find this less intimidating. You have to share a lot of the chinks in your own armor to get them to identify with you. You often have to go through the attorney, get permission, go to jail, be casual and relaxed."

Given the fact that these people are usually convicted killers, getting into a small room with them may make such advice hard to follow. But they can sense nervousness just as any other person would, so it is essential to remain relaxed and focused in your questioning while trying to win the trust on which candor is based. The format will be more straightforward because most social pleasantries have been removed in prison, but an approach based on honesty cuts through criminals' own natural duplicity. By telling them that they have the choice to be accurately represented in a book for the remainder of history in their own words, you are offering them the chance to straighten the record out. In appearing to be nonjudgmental about the charges against them and by offering the choice of cooperating, you are suggesting that they have a power over the situation that they really do not have. This may be directly at odds with the way in which you would deal with every other source, but it is an effective tactic in winning the cooperation of someone who is mentally unstable and highly dangerous.

"Criminals are tougher because they're psychos and they want to control everything. In face-to-face interviews, you've got to act like you like them," Jack Olsen says. "You've got to be somewhat hypocritical and be friendly no matter how repellent they are. What saves me is that I don't differentiate between people. We all start as seven, eight, or nine pounds of protoplasm and then all sorts of forces are brought to bear: social, genetic, educational, familial, sexual, and so on. That's what shapes people and their actions. I'm a determinist and I know that these people are the result of the forces that are inflicted upon them. I don't sit down with utter contempt for them. I mean, I hope that they're behind bars and I don't want them out, but I never think 'you rotten son of a bitch' when I sit down to interview them. I get in contact with the criminal however I can, through the attorney, the wife, the penitentiary officials, whoever has access. But you're dealing with psychopaths who like to run you and you have to be aware of it. You've got to have a great bullshit detector in this business and see through it, or you can get into trouble fast."

Chapter Five

NARRATING THE TRUE CRIME STORY

Beyond the Facts

Whether the medium is a book or a screenplay, the prospect of writing a true crime story can seem deceptively simple. On one hand there is a powerful, natural plot line implicit in the sequence of actions and events that led up to the commission of the crime. On the other, there is the challenge of weaving the seemingly endless details that your research has produced into a narrative that will grip the readers' attention and keep them turning the pages. But after all, if you already have a tragic event, a suspenseful plot, a cast of characters, and a dramatic outcome, how hard can it be to put it together? In a word, "very."

The challenge of true crime writing is the same in all forms of creative nonfiction. Often called the "literature of reality," this approach embodies the accurate, factual detail of journalism with the narrative structure of a fictional account. In part, its appeal comes from the way it allows readers to get inside the minds and motives of characters and experience the atmosphere of a physical setting rather than just work their way through a chronology of events and facts. Creative nonfiction enables readers to immerse themselves in another world—one that they would be afraid to venture into in the course of their daily lives—and deal with people who might normally terrify them. The best of this type of writing will offer the pacing, texture, and drama of a well-crafted novel, but will still stand up to the rigors of both standard journalistic ethics and the professional paranoia of a publisher's or studio's legal department.

The trick is to know when to employ basic reportorial skills and when to portray events and frame dialogue like a novelist. If you simply try to string together all your research in the same way a newspaper reporter would, you will wind up with a dry recounting of the facts. While this will be accurate to a fault, chances are it will also be boring. But if you stray too far into the realm of fictional techniques, you may wind up with an interesting story that is potentially libelous or will simply lack the gravity of truth that every true crime reader demands.

"What people don't realize is that these are not easy books to write," says editor Michaela Hamilton. "Badly executed true crime books tend to be very repetitious:

You have the crime, somebody discovers it, the investigation follows the trail of the killer, the trial, the penalty phase, and so on. It's a challenge for the writer to structure it in a way that is not boring, one that skillfully releases the information. I need writers who can do research and do narrative writing and that's tough because journalists can do the research but often can't develop a narrative. That's because writing a four-thousand-word story is different from a ninety-thousand-word book. While I often have to give them really detailed editorial guidance, I've found that novelists who are crossing over are just the opposite. They know a good story, but don't know how to do the research, work with sources, or get people to open up in an interview."

This combination of skills is essential because the basis of the genre's appeal is its ability to capture the extremes of human behavior. Researching deeply and effectively will ultimately provide you with more freedom when it comes time to put the story on the page because you will have an innate command of the facts involved. Solid and repeated interviews will enable you to capture your characters' spirits, attitudes, and expressions in a way that reveals them to a reader. Where traditional journalism requires a writer to *describe* real people, places, and events in the course of telling a story, creative nonfiction allows you to *re-create* them. In doing so, you bring them to life by enlarging the meaning and impact of their actions, thoughts, and feelings in a way that readers can absorb—especially if it is something or someone that would normally repulse or terrify them. The more twisted the motivation and depraved the violence, the more fascinated people are. But first you have to get them to believe in both the story and the characters.

"That's the key to good crime writing, to be able to do incredible research and immerse yourself in it to the point where you dream about it," explains Mary Ann Lynch of Macmillan. "In the best examples of the genre, people are immersed and so involved that the other world is yours and that carries onto the page. That's what people want—to be taken into another world and learn about it—and the unsuccessful books are those that are formulaic and flat and don't involve the reader. The best true crime writing has a pulse that takes you with it and carries you away into another world and that's what I look for when considering a project. True crime does what criminals do—it seduces you into believing and not wanting to walk away even though you know something horrible will happen."

But to achieve this, you must be sensitive to several issues. While you are often omnipotent, moving viewpoints in and out of characters, providing background descriptions, and splicing timelines to keep the action moving forward, you must never project yourself into a story. Just as in an interview with a convicted killer, every hint of judgment must be withheld. It should always be the motivation and actions of the individuals involved that create the drama and suspense of events, not you. Your writing should never stereotype your characters, make them into clichés, or let them reflect your opinions. When it comes to true crime, readers want the writer to disappear and the story to flow seamlessly from one plot twist to another.

"I want a writer who has the ability to select the relevant facts from a lot of information, and is able to tell the story in a clear and dramatic way. People are going to read this book for information it contains as well as the story. A problem occurs when a writer injects themselves into the story because you lose the objectivity of the story. This is particularly true of people who fancy themselves part of the New School of journalism," says Paul Dinas of Kensington. "But the readers don't care about the writer—they care about the story and [the writer] can get in the way 'cause it tips the scale."

In many cases, you can avoid this tendency by writing the story in scenes. This is a fiction-oriented technique that *shows* rather than *tells* the reader what is going on to advance the story. It combines a specific setting, characters, and dialogue or action in a way that conveys information by making the reader feel present and involved as the plot evolves toward a conclusion. Scenes are great for capturing emotions or key moments of decision or portraying conflict between characters. They are the opposite of the journalistic staple of recounting the facts, because they let readers experience the season or the smell of an old gas station while watching an argument between two old friends degenerate into murder. If you're truly focused on making the scene come to life on the page, there is a strong chance you'll keep your own feelings out of the picture because they will just be in the way.

The Lead

One of the most effective ways to manage an expansive research effort is through the use of a chronology. But this approach is also helpful when you're finally sitting down to write. Not only does it provide an entire timeline for the story, but it also helps you see where subplots develop along the way. This basic structure can then be used to foreshadow events with details that hint—but don't reveal—what is to come. But that doesn't necessarily mean that every story has to start at the beginning. In fact, when it comes to true crime, an expository lead to a story is often enough to make the reader put it down.

Part of the appeal of true crime is the innate suspense that comes with the knowledge that *something* is always about to happen, but not knowing what, where, or when it will occur. At its most elemental, the genre has all the classic lines of a Greek tragedy. There is the central event of the crime, the hunt or quest of the investigation, the climax as the criminal is apprehended, and the catharsis of the trial where justice is served. This is the elemental dramatic structure of Western literature, but its effectiveness has become limited in true crime writing due to overuse and the changing tastes of the public. Television has altered the way people develop and sustain interest in a story and attention spans in general have been reduced. This has been accompanied by the rise of a more tabloid approach to presenting the news and the combination that tends to catch people's notice is one of provocative sensationalism. But sensational leads can often undercut the impact of a true story and it is far wiser to try to catch someone's attention by being provocative or offering teasing hints of what is to come.

"True crime can be much wilder than fiction because you couldn't make some of that stuff up. In either case, I believe that if you're a storyteller at heart, you know how best to tell a story," says Edna Buchanan. "The beginnings are the most important because we live in an age where attention spans are very short, so you have to get up front. A lot of times, I'll tell the story to a friend or a neighbor and then, just by hearing it out loud, I'd be able to get the lead. Or it will come to me while I'm driving or in the shower or wherever. The lead is really important and the first line is always the most important thing. It should be both provocative and informational. You have to be fair with the reader and not try to grab them with some line that is there for some sort of sensationalism, but you always have to keep them reading. I always like to have sharp leads, because as a reporter I found that so many readers never followed the jump of a story to the back pages. So I learned to make a point—to write the stories in a way where you have to go along with the flow—early in my career."

One of the classic risks in writing true crime is to front-load your lead by providing too much information too soon. This is often a problem for journalists who favor the classic pyramid lead structure that informs the readers of the elements of "who, what, when, where, why, and how" before they get into the substance of the story. While this structure is highly effective as a mechanism for reporting a story, it fails when it comes to telling one. Developed to inform readers quickly, it allows people to skim a piece to determine their interest in reading on. If this happens in the opening of a true crime story, it is the writer who is dead.

"I have a good idea where I'm going when I start to write. The first third of the book is the toughest and I can often spend five months getting the initial chapters right," says Lowell Cauffiel. "Right up front I write a section in a way that implies all sorts of things, usually through a scene that encapsulates the book like a giant thesis statement and hints at what's to come. I like to build to the crime. Everything I put in has to reinforce the plot, every detail must advance the plot, and that's a mistake a lot of budding nonfiction writers make, not understanding how to use details appropriately. I always develop my characters throughout the entire book and they aren't fully revealed until the final pages. A tendency among many writers is to front-load the book with an entire chapter about someone's past and then move on to someone or something else. That just spends the capital up front. Part of the suspense, mystery, and appeal of true crime writing is the ability to hook the readers and compel them to read all the way through to the end. It's much more effective that way. I love when people tell me they read the last chapter first and didn't get anything from it. That means I'm doing it right."

But techniques differ widely. Some writers will start by writing the ending first and then use that as a reference point through which they can frame their lead. Others will start chronologically, wait until a subplot develops, and then magnify that and reorient it as a point of entry into a story that already seems to be moving. Some will use a sense of place or setting to capture interest, particularly if it is highly unusual, but this often requires very strong skills. The classic technique is to use action, to make the characters come alive in ways that hint at their motives or the forces that shape them. In the words of Jack Olsen, "There used to be an old rule in true crime writing—'Drop the body through the roof to get their attention with action right from the start.'" While this may be overstating the case, Olsen does have a point and most successful true crime writers haven't missed it.

"Although I began with a body in *The Hillside Stranglers,* it's the only book that I've started that way. I used that approach only because there were so many bodies involved in the story that I felt I had to," says Darcy

O'Brien. "But I really feel you have to hook the audience with action scenes and get the background in through incidents. In my next book, which has a great first chapter, I used a sense of place because the area in southern Illinois was so gothic and fascinating. The people were mean and there's a bizarre history of gangsters, outlaw caves, and even a serial killer in the eighteenth century. It was great to set the reader in the place and let the story unfold, just like *In Cold Blood* does. But the writing is so strong that you don't notice that nothing is going on."

Sometimes a sense of action and interest can be advanced through the shifting of timelines. Events and characters can be quickly juxtaposed right from the start, creating a sense of movement and evolving motives while not revealing pivotal information in a way that makes the readers feel as if they already know how the story will turn out. This approach can be effective because it immediately establishes the interrelation between characters and events that, on the surface, would appear to be totally disconnected. The result is a story that has a quick pace and the natural draw of keeping the readers interested until they can see how these two strands will eventually come together.

"I started off with the crime and that's the formula and I wouldn't do that again—it's too uncreative," Harry MacLean says. "In my second book I had to present the psychology of the family, so I ran two timelines at once right from the start—present and past—and weaved them in and out in a rhythm so they wouldn't get too bored. The use of flashbacks is a common technique, but if it's done well it can really work."

Characters and Dialogue

The main result of all primary research efforts is to develop an extensive knowledge of the individuals involved in the commission and resolution of a violent crime. In the end, you may know about their youthful achievements as a student or as an athlete, the sad details of a broken marriage or a secret affair, a hidden criminal record, or a string of illicit business deals. But not everything needs to be revealed for a story to be successful. When it comes to writing, it is the selection of facts and actions you choose to use that creates a character in a reader's mind. This is pivotal to the success of your story because no matter how horrific the crime or how thrilling the chase of the criminal, readers who cannot identify with the characters won't go much further than the lead.

"After you get all this information, one of the big challenges when it comes to writing is how do you make the people interesting," says Harry MacLean. "Sometimes there's a natural tension between good and evil in the personalities, but if it isn't there you have to create it. You have to make the reader care about one of the characters by making one of them sympathetic. Capote made people care about the bad guy. In my first book, I made the community itself the sympathetic character. A lot of stories will lack a good strong hero or a sympathetic character and if you can't figure out how to magnify someone's appealing traits, you will have a dumb story, a newspaper piece. That's the skill a writer brings to the story and it is something that has to be a conscious effort right from the beginning. You have to spin the trail out in a way that involves the reader, a way that characterizes a person's background that doesn't take away from the narrative. If you set your hook well enough up front, the reader will cut you a lot of slack."

In some respects, strong characters can outweigh the importance of a strong story. If a reader doesn't like or can't identify with at least one of the primary characters involved, it won't matter how good or unusual the overall plot line is. This is because every true crime story is, at its heart, a human interest story. People use the actions and reactions of characters that have been placed in unusual circumstances as a yardstick of their own behavior. They project their own strengths and weaknesses, their own moral judgments, onto the actions of individual characters. Inasmuch as the vicarious sensation of thinking "There but for the grace of God go I" when reading about an awful crime creates a sense of interest, all readers wonder how they would react when confronted with the darkness of violence and the choices between right and wrong.

"To the readers, the true crime story offers a character check for themselves because they want to know what made these people commit these acts," Lowell Cauffiel explains. "These books allow them to explore a natural fear in themselves. Deep inside they're afraid that they may one day commit a crime or a murder and they want to know what makes them different from these people. As a writer, my goal is to really disturb the reader—to access their emotions, to tell a story that brings these feelings out. My books take readers to a place they cannot normally get to and the stories reveal not only the motives and actions of the key participants, but also a bigger theme that is part of the American experience. They also tend to emphasize people who appear to be one thing, but are really something completely different underneath. That's what drove me to write *Masquerade*. Although he appeared to be someone who was normal, the main character was obsessed and in the grip of dark forces. I wanted to know what made people want to destroy themselves, why they go over the edge. I had been close enough to those things myself, but I lived and went on. I found that it boiled down to choices: The choices people make are what determine their destiny. That's what these books are about—the choices people make and the impact of those decisions on their lives and the lives of others. That's something that people can relate to and the number one person in my mind is the reader. The reader has to be able to identify with these characters because as you 'peel the onion' of their personality throughout the book, the contrast between the horror inside and their outward appearance is that much more powerful."

But the writer's challenge often boils down to how to effectively reveal the inner nature of the characters and the forces that are driving their behavior. While a journalist can describe people and their backgrounds in an expository fashion, this can be a hazard for the true crime writer, especially early on in the development of a story, because the least effective stories are those that rely heavily on description. This approach makes characters appear as cardboard figures who are marched in and out of scenes at the whim of the writer. As in fiction, characters in creative nonfiction stories are most effectively revealed through their statements and actions as the story progresses. This enables them to assume a distinct identity while also making the development of the plot appear to be a direct result of their behavior. But the true crime writer faces a quandary. While actions can reveal a character and advance a plot, they cannot always explain underlying motives or background issues that are essential to making actions and statements believable.

"One of my rules is that you've got to show the subject in action to get the readers involved in both the character and the story," says Jack Olsen. "You've got to hook them until they are so interested that you can give them ten pages of background and they won't mind it. It might take forty pages to get them to that point where they are asking 'where'd this guy come from?'—but then you're ready to get to the interesting part. You've got to show your characters doing interesting things and make sure that they're interesting people before you can get into the expository biography and off the main narrative. You've got to show the guy in action so the reader *wants* the description."

To get the reader to this critical point, most writers drive their characters' actions through dialogue or direct quotations. Crisp exchanges between the people involved in the story or a simple statement can eliminate much of the need for description. Whether it is through accents, humor, or the emotional content of a conversation, dialogue and quotes reveal characters and bring them to life in a way that the most accomplished expository writing never will. In fact, once someone's character has been established in the reader's mind, what they often *don't* say can be as revealing as what they do because effective dialogue always has an emotional content.

Dialogue and quotations come directly from your research. Whether it is from an interview, a police report, a news article, or a trial transcript, every statement has to be accurate in both its content and depiction of the character. In the case of a quotation, this is usually not a problem because it comes either directly from the person who spoke it or from a record of the statement. But it is impossible to write dialogue without re-creating it and this has long been a bane of true crime writers. An accurate re-creation often takes tracking down multiple sources and then comparing versions of what was said and how it was said. One of the reasons so many writers will repeatedly interview the same subjects about the same conversations or events is to establish a sense of accuracy, but the other is to capture the tone and delivery of the intent behind the words.

"With the cops and prosecutors, I wait till the case is over so they can relax because everything's on the public record and they can talk about it," says Ann Rule. "Every time I start a book, I'm always terrified that I'll never find out enough because it's often about secrets that people have hidden for years. But I stay with it and it's amazing what will turn up if you stay there long enough. When people know that you really care, they will tell you anything. If someone says 'Don't use this,' I won't. But everyone has a story to tell and they love to have an audience. I usually use a tape recorder and I'm always amazed at how many people will let you do that. I prefer to use tape because I like to have absolutely accurate quotes but I don't transcribe them. I just listen to them, especially during long car rides. I listen to them over and over so they become part of my consciousness.

Unfortunately, no matter how long it has been since a case was resolved, many people still won't talk to you at first. Part of it can be shame, part can be pain, and part can simply be the deep and abiding desire to forget and let go. As a result, many writers will use pseudonyms as a means of offering protection to their sources while gaining the access they need to corroborate some statement or conversation. But in many cases, especially when the victim was involved in the action, it is impossible to write authentic dialogue or statements. In those instances, you must check as many sources as possible and simply paraphrase what was said.

"I will make up names in some cases where people are sensitive about their identities," says Darcy O'Brien. "Paraphrasing can be done to re-create conversations, but I try to use that kind of dialogue only when it expresses the characters and their manner of speech, not for expository information. I will study patterns of speech from tapes and notes and, if you have two or three witnesses to a conversation, I think it's okay to replicate it. But I would never write anything like that without having spoken to one of the people who was part of the conversation."

Setting

While characters and dialogue go a long way in moving a story toward its conclusion, the physical setting of a crime also plays an important role. The details of a place can subtly unveil issues such as social status, local or regional cultural influences that may shape a character's motives, or the highly compartmentalized nature of someone's secret life. Although extensive description is something to be avoided because it can distract from character development and offset the impact of direct action, a well-placed re-creation of a setting can have a strong influence on a reader's perception of events.

"I use maps a lot and I have a program in my computer that will give me the topographic nature of the area and the street layout," says Ann Rule. "I also use weather reports and one of my favorite things is to go back to the crime scene and use a timeline book that will help re-create the era. I always go to the place where things will happen so the reader can see it through my eyes. It all adds up."

Beyond framing the actions of the characters, setting can help add color and texture to a story. Characters can display personal interests and aversions or compulsive or destructive behaviors. But in the hands of a skilled writer, a setting can be so powerful that it can equal the actions of the people in it. It can make the readers feel at home with the seasons of the year, the rhythms of local life, and the dynamics of local institutions such as churches, PTAs, or social clubs, boosting their emotional response to the situation. Perhaps the most powerful example in the genre can be seen in the opening of *In Cold Blood,* where Capote creates such a powerful sense of place that it heightens the brutality of the killings that were to occur.

"I think you can get a place through someone's eyes, but you also have to describe the countryside at some point," says Harry MacLean. "To show how the people in my first book were tied into the land and the weather, I ran the planting and harvesting cycle throughout the story. It became like a character itself. That way the place came alive. But it has to be something other than simple description, so I used the actions of planting, growing, and harvesting the crop. The nature of the town—the way those people lived, and the forces that shaped their lives—was critical to the heart of the story and the crime that was committed there."

Writing True Crime Screenplays

One of the great myths is that true crime is *written* for television or feature films. It is not. True crime is always *adapted*—and these days the medium is almost exclusively television. Whether the story comes from a book or directly from field research and working with the people involved, it is the adaptation of real life into a medium that has very little to do with real life. The basic elements of a story will remain the same, but the format of a medium such as film or video means that everything has to happen through action and dialogue within an unnaturally short amount of time—two hours at the most. This requires that timelines be compressed and characters composited to fit in the space provided. The result, particularly for writers who are committed to recreating the atmosphere and dynamics of reality as accurately as possible, is often disappointing.

This is not to say that true crime movies are not truthful, because the producers involved also share an abiding interest in telling a true story. In fact, both they and the networks that air their work are dedicated to it—if only for legal reasons. But there are often limits to the language that can be used on television, and the format has a very rigid structure that predetermines pacing and plot points. In a movie, you've got to make things happen quickly, and subtlety is often wasted or simply not wanted because action is the byword of success.

"The biggest problem with an adaptation is to find a story with an active central character because in most true stories the central character is not overtly active," says producer Janet Faust-Krusi. "In life, most people go through an emotional journey that is reactive to outside events and that journey is internal. But for film you need a character who is active because everything happens through action and dialogue. The other issue is that real life rarely fits neatly into a seven-act structure. An event or a transformation of a character might have taken place over twenty-four hours or ten years. It never happens in two hours. So you have to compress or expand time while remaining true to the dynamics of the story. That's what a lot of people don't understand, especially the people whose story is being adapted."

This requires an entirely different logic and approach when it comes to writing. In fact, many writers who have been very successful as journalists or authors fail miserably when trying to deal with the constraints of the adaptation process, because the tools that have served them so well for so long are not applicable in this medium. It's not that they aren't skilled, it's just that skills of a different type are required. Unlike a book, the beginning of a movie has to be front-loaded to generate interest. Then plot points are specifically charted to match commercial breaks and to keep the audience from turning the dial. Many print writers feel that this structure limits their creativity when it comes to choosing points of view or the pacing of the narrative. Given the divergence of skills, most producers have found it easier to hire the original writer as a consultant and use someone who exclusively works on adaptations to write the script itself.

"Adapting true stories to television has its own problems because television operates on a seven-act structure, one that is filled with interruptions," says producer Frank von Zurnick, who has adapted over a hundred stories for television. "So by the end of act one, about twenty-five minutes into the hour, you have to have the theme out there and establish what the essential conflict is. By the third act, which should come right at the ten o'clock hour where the viewer has the chance to change the channel, you have to have a plot turn that drives the second hour of the movie right to the end. Feature films are different because the audience is a prisoner so you can wait until the end of the second act or into the third before turning up the heat.

"The biggest challenge when adapting is not to inject your own subjective viewpoints about the story. When this happens it can often be to the detriment of what really happened. We usually have to compress timelines and characters to maintain the dramatic pace required by the format, but the point of view has to be really balanced to make it work. That's one of the reasons we use writers who specialize in adaptations."

Chapter Six

SECONDARY RESEARCH AND LIABILITY ISSUES

Covering Your Tracks

W hat makes the best true crime writing different from other nonfiction genres is the writer's abiding commitment to uncovering the truth that unites a complex tale of often irrational behavior. But unraveling a story that is by nature unpleasant and often filled with horrible violence, hidden lives, and long-kept secrets is always a difficult prospect. Emotions run high, people feel protective, and the truth is often considered to be a malleable subject, one highly dependent on point of view and colored by the speaker's relationship to the victim. Whether by intent, neglect, or the simple erosion of time on memory, multiple versions of the same event collected during the research phase can be radically different. That's one of the reasons the police are always reluctant about prosecuting a case where the primary piece of evidence is an eyewitness account. People can forget, they can misconstrue, or they can tell the story over so many times that it changes and takes on a life of its own, one that can be more dramatic than the actual event or changes their relationship to it. Unfortunately, errors or omissions in the final version a writer produces can cause further damage to the lives of the people caught up in the aftermath of a crime just as easily as they can open up the author, publisher, or production company to legal liabilities. What's more, a misrepresentation of the facts can distort the perceptions of the readers, damage their impression of the genre, and ruin the writer's reputation.

While a highly detailed account of a crime helps provide color and depth to a narrative, the need for accuracy is one of the driving forces behind such an exhaustive approach to researching every case. By constantly cross-checking facts, quotes, and the sequence of events, a writer will wind up with an objective overview of what really happened, who did what, and when they did it. While most of this information is available through legal records or can be extracted by a skillful interviewer, potential problems remain. One is the issue of ethics and investigative techniques; the other is creative license in writing about a case after the fact, in which some of the characters are dead.

There are always occasions when there will be the temptation to access information in a manner that may or may not be ethical. As a matter of course, journalists are trained in codes of ethics when they work in a newsroom or for a magazine. Some of these are obvious: Never accept free meals, gifts, or trips from a source; never plagiarize another writer's work; never make up facts, statistics, or quotes; never make promises that you can't keep in exchange for information; never entrap or blackmail a source into divulging information. But other lines of professional behavior are less clear or subject to what have become known as "situational ethics." Should you ambush a subject you need to interview but who has refused to talk to you? Should you always identify yourself as a writer when someone brings up the case you are covering in conversation? Should you always identify a source? What do you do when trying to recreate a conversation with someone who is long dead? Should you change a character's name or the location of a crime?

Beyond considering the direct legal ramifications, one of the time-honored approaches used by journalists when trying to answer questions such as these is to put themselves on the other end of the equation. That is, to ask "How would I feel if . . . ?" This is both a philosophical and practical exercise, but it does not always answer every question. In fact, practices that are legal may not always be ethical when it comes to investigative writing. Perhaps this is why so many writers are quick to cite the law or the constitution as a defense for what may be questionable behavior. In any case, all true crime writers owe it to themselves, their profession, and the genre to be as fair, accurate, and thorough as possible in their work.

Still, it is important to realize that being in the business of writing the truth will probably earn you the enmity of someone involved in the case. People always have their version of the facts and the story and it may not match the one that a thorough research effort uncovers. Major crimes, particularly murders, also tend to involve people who are mentally or emotionally unstable. When they disagree with a writer's version of events, they often file a lawsuit—or take direct action.

"I have received death threats plenty of times, but the people who scare me are on death row so I don't worry too much," says Darcy O'Brien. "But you really can't help but offend people when you write the truth. If someone warns me not to go into a certain area or the police or the FBI tell me not to go someplace unless they went with me, I take that seriously. This is especially true when you investigate anything related to narcotics, which is pretty much everything these days."

It should be noted that O'Brien is not alone. Virtually every writer interviewed for this book maintains a low profile when not covering a case. All have unlisted phone numbers and impersonal e-mail addresses, most live in remote areas with a post office box as an address and only allow articles or book jackets to mention the region (say, "the Northwest") where they are located—and some sleep with a gun, just in case.

Accuracy

Since many readers love the genre for its entertainment value as well as its literary merit, few people look to the true crime writer in the same manner in which they would regard a newspaper journalist when it comes to the issue of accountability. Many people simply believe that "if it is in print, it must be true" and construe a book or an adapted screenplay as a direct and actual representation of history. Although not responsible for how people interpret their work, writers remain responsible for the accuracy of the content of it. Even though some creative license is involved in developing a narrative, no details should be invented, particularly when they are known or available through research. The writer should never invent major facts that may change the course of the story.

"Invented detail does not belong in a true crime book. Invented or re-created conversation is an accepted technique in creative nonfiction and is perfectly acceptable in a true crime book provided that the research and sources can back it up," says editor Michaela Hamilton. "It is often necessary for the narrative, but it has to be accurate. The authors are responsible for accuracy for the book. Although we provide a legal reading for libel and intellectual property rights and privacy issues, an author is responsible for accuracy. They have to turn in an accurate manuscript to begin, then double-check it through the copyediting and galley stages."

Given the tabloid and pulp roots of American true crime writing, the issue of accuracy has always been a thorny one for the genre. Even Capote's modern classic *In Cold Blood* was tainted right from the start by its freely admitted use of "faction" as a means of dramatizing the story. It is widely accepted that Capote fabricated whole sections of conversation and even the book's ending to achieve his narrative goals. While this made for brilliant reading, it also put an enormous burden on subsequent true crime narratives because, by and large, the public believed that Capote's book was entirely truthful and accurate and that every other book in the genre should match it for narrative style. Unfortunately, while they can be dramatic in their own right, few stories based completely in the truth are as riveting as one that borrows freely from both fact and fiction to advance the plot. These days, it is accepted that anything a writer does add or invent to a true crime story must be based on existing but incomplete factual knowledge about a person or place; it cannot be fabricated from imagination.

This controversy over where the line between fact and "faction" lies in true crime became particularly heated following the recent success of *Sleepers*, Lorenzo Carcaterra's huge bestseller. Jack Olsen has been quite public in his claims that the work is "a total hoax that has been shown up and down that there aren't three consecutive words in that story that are true" despite the author's claims to the contrary. The swirl of highly public criticism around this controversy has, in part, led to a swing back toward more established journalistic techniques in the genre. Now more than ever, writers are going the extra mile to make sure that their material is accurate and honest.

"I check everything from brand names of things to weather reports of the time and place of events," says Lowell Cauffiel. "If I get an allegation about someone or something, I try to get multiple sources but try to stay away from attribution unless I can confirm something. As a rule, the legal standard is 'a reasonable facsimile thereof' when re-creating dialogue, but I try to go one step further. I spend so much time with these people and I tape them, trying to get their exact words and tone. Then I will run it back by the other person who was in the conversation and see if they agree with it. I won't go with one person's version unless the other is dead."

Creative License

As Cauffiel astutely points out, the issue of accuracy in recreating dialogue becomes a gray area that is tricky to navigate because some of the characters in every true crime story are dead. That brings the issue of creative license into question when re-creating conversations and events because, despite a deep commitment to accuracy, every writer must develop an approach to dealing with missing details and sources that are necessary to make a narrative compelling. This is a tricky issue and it can be resolved in a number of ways. Many writers try to balance any license they have taken in a note in the acknowledgments section or in a foreword that addresses potential questions about their technique or research. Others will use an asterisk or a footnote or italics. Whatever approach you choose, the general consensus is that you need to signal where and when you filled in a blank to keep the story moving.

"I've never made anything up like Capote did. After all, the family members that he quoted were dead," says Harry MacLean. "I always re-create with some direct knowledge of what took place at the time. But if it was a secondary or tertiary event, I would indicate it in some way. You have to be careful, and what people say in the foreword about how they did the research and where they took license is always interesting because it alerts the reader that you're making some stuff up, which is potentially hazardous to your credibility. If it's obvious, it doesn't matter. I'm very careful because I want every fact in there if someone ever challenges me. Whether it is an editor or another journalist, or a lawsuit, I want to be able to cite sources."

But questions still remain. What if the source has been dead for years? Or what if it is a pivotal conversation, one that indicates intent or a plan of action or a fear of what is to come and is central to the plot of a story and you only have one side of the story?

"When it comes to dialogue, sometimes you have to make part of it up because someone is gone and can't confirm what they said," says Jack Olsen. "You can, but those sections can't be significant and it has to be true, to be based on what you were told. I don't use anything like that unless one of the people in the conversation tells me what was said and I won't use anything that's been overheard. The person telling me has to have been one of the people involved in the conversation."

At the risk of generalizing, most true crime readers don't care about small embellishments on a physical description that sets a scene or clarifies a re-created conversation. This is true as long as it doesn't libel someone or misconstrue the facts. In fact, most people can't remember the exact phrasing of a conversation they had with a friend the week before or what they were wearing when they had it. Readers are reasonable in this regard and won't object to something they read unless it strikes them as illogical that the writer would know it. In fact, in many cases writers will find that legally deposed recollections of what was said are very inexact and only the overall intent, time, and place of the conversation have stayed with the people who were there. In such instances, a writer will have to fill in the blanks while remaining true to the intent of what was said. But just to be sure, some writers will go a step further.

"One thing I always do is promise my detective and the victim's family that they can read every word I write before it goes to press. I'm the writer, so they can't control me or lead me, but since they were there and they lived it, they'll let me know if I'm not re-creating it truthfully," explains Jay Fletcher. "This is important because it can be easy to get a wrong impression about an event that happened and then incorporate it into the text. I do this to make sure I re-create the story they tried to tell me as accurately as possible. This also gives me some of the creative license I need to re-create scenes because people don't care about exact words as much as they care about tone and intent of what is said. When I make that promise, those words seems to sweep away their last reservations about the fact that you, a stranger, won't go off and write something that is inaccurate and will ruin their lives. It may seem to be a small thing, but it has given me much better books than I would have had if I hadn't been willing to do it."

Changing Names

The rules get a little looser when it comes to changing the name of a character or characters represented in a story. Often this is done to protect a source or someone's privacy, but in many cases it is done because people will not cooperate without being assured that their real name won't appear. As long as there is a disclaimer that informs the reader, this is an accepted practice in mainstream journalism and it is widely practiced in true crime writing. Given the potential risks and danger to an individual who is revealing secrets or facts about a murder or major crime, most readers don't even bat an eye when they are informed that a name has been changed.

"I don't mind changing names because a lot of people won't cooperate unless you do that," says Jack Olsen. "When I wrote *Son*, I started sticking an asterisk next to a changed name the first time it was used, and a lot of people will do this or italicize the name the first time it appears. What you want to do as a writer is to hold the explanations to a minimum and the reader doesn't really care anyway, especially if you let them know what you are doing. But if you change the timeline or take liberty with a quote, you have to let the reader know and as long as you're honest on that level, you can have a lot of latitude in how you shape a story."

Prepublication Review

In light of the potential liability involved in writing true crime, every story must undergo an extensive prepublication review to vet it and eliminate problems. This process is typically broken down into two distinct phases. The first review is handled by the writer; the second by a publisher.

Like Jay Fletcher, some writers will offer their main sources for a story the chance to read through the manuscript for issues of accuracy. This is often helpful in ensuring that the intent of people's actions and words has been captured accurately, but it can sometimes add new information on a subject. This may sound surprising, but it is amazing what people can remember when they see an entire story laid out in front of them. New facts can come to light at this stage that will enhance the narrative. However, it is essential that anyone reviewing the manuscript in this manner understand that they are doing so for issues of accuracy only; if they find something that is clearly inaccurate, it will be changed. Everything else is to be considered a matter of opinion or a request for a change that will be cross-checked against the sources and material in your research files. If it comes to an issue where the interpretation of a quote or the context of a situation is at stake, you may want to reveal the source of the quote or the description of an event—a tape or a transcript—to clarify it.

As a rule, this tends to be more of a problem with depictions of conversations than sequences of events because words are harder to remember than actions. While many writers are reluctant to use tape recorders in interview situations, tapes are extremely helpful when it comes to fact checking. Remember, the material being quoted may not be used until a year or two after the conversation takes place and—unlike a notebook—a tape is free from a writer's interpretative bias.

"I usually tape my interviews for the purpose of accuracy because everything I write goes in front of lawyers and the tapes keep them at bay when you are having the manuscript vetted," explains Fred Rosen. "You have an indemnity clause in the publishing contract that releases them from any lawsuits by anyone who is quoted in the book. But most people who sue go after the deep pockets of the publisher and the only way you can avoid that is by being meticulous."

The review phase can be made easier if you have created a source chronology and index as suggested in Chapter 3. When you have a comprehensive list of where material came from, the prospect of running down sources becomes far less daunting. Such a list also facilitates dealing with any challenges from a publisher's lawyer or threats from lawyers representing a source that feels maligned.

Still, it is amazing what people can object to and no amount of vetting can completely eliminate the possibility of legal action. Some journalists insist on a line-by-line review of their stories to check for the use of minor descriptive phrases that may be misconstrued, but that is rarely feasible when writing a true crime narrative. Often it is not the issue of whether or not something is true, but whether someone has been portrayed as "ugly" or "conniving" or "deceitful." While this may be a simple statement of fact and the writer may have a wealth of material to back it up, few people would readily reach for such words to describe themselves. In most cases, legal actions come from peripheral characters who object to their portrayal in a story.

"Usually I will sign a writer up, get the manuscript by the due date, edit it, do any revisions, and then send it to our legal department," says Charles Spicer. "That is the very important part because it's usually not the principal people who will sue, it's always the minor characters. The legal department vets it from libel issues and anything that may be questioned in regard to truthfulness. It seems to work because we've never been sued over one of our true crime books."

Spicer's luck notwithstanding, the simple fact of the matter is that we live in a highly litigious society. It is easy for someone to sue a writer over something in a book, particularly if the book is successful or the case has a high profile. Sometimes people want attention, other times they want to deflect public criticism of their character or behavior. But even without merit, every suit has to be dealt with and that costs time and money. To neutralize this, virtually every true crime book goes through an extensive legal review paid for by the publisher. These companies typically spend between $5,000 and $7,000 on such a review and it can be harrowing for the unprepared writer, but it is considered an essential part of the process.

"All my books have legal reads. If you're a big corporation you have a lot of exposure and people always go after the deep pockets," Mary Ann Lynch explains. "People feel that they can come after you and big companies don't want to be involved in lawsuits because of the expense. Even with a nuisance suit. The cost of a legal read before you go to press is nothing in comparison to the costs of that kind of suit."

Movies and Television

When a book or story is sold to a movie or television producer, it is often transformed as a result of being adapted to another form of medium. Many writers have found that years of hard work and dedication to incorporating the most minute of details are lost in the adaptation process. That is not to say that gross liberties are taken in retelling the story, but that the method of telling it on a screen is substantially different from the one used in a book. Techniques such as interior dialogue and description have no place in a screenplay, where everything has to be shown either through action or dialogue between characters. Also, the time constraints—an hour or a two-hour format, often with commercial interruptions—usually means that characters, timelines, or events have to be compressed to dramatize them effectively.

The most popular screen format for a true crime story is a television movie of the week or miniseries. Every network has extensive legal departments who are concerned with several areas of liability. Errors and Omissions (E&O) department attorneys are concerned with problems of accuracy and being sued by misrepresentations of characters or the events surrounding them. The primary way around these issues is to buy the rights to the story from both the writer and the principal people involved in it. This allows producers to make dramatic alterations to the story without fear of being sued.

In addition to timeline and format issues, these adjustments are often necessary because the pace of real lives and events rarely fits neatly into the structure required for television.

The alternative to buying the rights from the principals involved would be to have two sources for everything that is quoted in the script or anything that may make the network or the production company potentially liable. This was the standard approach used in docudramas where real names and real events were used, but now it is far more common to buy the rights to a story. While producers and directors are as concerned with accuracy as the next professional, the issue is often one of expediency. In the highly competitive world of film making, it is faster and easier to spend the money on rights and eliminate any potential problems up front than it is to develop a bullet-proof index of secondary sources. Still, the final script is always reviewed by the network before production begins.

"You have an obligation to the movie, the network, and the people involved, to be accurate and truthful," says producer Janet Faust-Krusi. "We have to hand in a very detailed script to the network's legal department to be vetted, and while you can make dramatic adjustments, you have to stay pretty true to the story for legal reasons. But there is a difficulty in turning something into a dramatic story that works on TV. In many ways, I think it's more difficult than starting to write something from scratch because you have to be accountable to the network, to the people whose story it is, and to your own attorneys so that you don't get hit with a lawsuit."

The other review that networks and studios insist on is by the Standards and Practices (S&P) department. This review often focuses on the level of violence or gore that goes into an adaptation and S&P lawyers think nothing of weighing in and cutting out elements of story based on perceived moral or image issues. In more direct terms, they are often less concerned with what it takes to tell the story correctly than the issue of who will be angry with the network and give it bad press following release.

While book writers might not like what happens to a story once it is sold to Hollywood, they must understand the nature of the adaptive process. Rather than an actual depiction of facts, the adapted story maintains a certain geometry of them—who did what to whom and why and when—within a rigidly structured plot line. Writers who do adaptations have to get the dynamics down within that structure: Reveal what the problem is in the first act, then make it worse in the second act, and resolve it in the third—with allowances for commercial breaks en route. This means that characters and facts get compressed into one person or one scene to capture the essence of the story while remaining true to the main drama of it.

"With a book, a writer works by himself and with an editor. In film, a writer has to hand over his work to directors and actors and producers, all of whom have to bend their efforts to the medium because the end product is pictures, not words," says Brian Lane, a long-time television writer and author of *Cat and Mouse*. "The writer winds up having his material being translated by a number of people because there is no such thing as a direct translation from one medium to another. A film is a different animal than a book, and it changes everything. I think that's one of the reasons that true crime writers are often so disappointed when they see their work adapted, because they see it as it really was and the dynamics of film demands that it appear as something else."

Producers are aware of this as well, which is one of the reasons they tend to use writers who specialize in adaptations rather than the original writer when it comes time to develop a screenplay. Although they usually hire the author as a consultant to check facts and the overall dynamic of the script, this role is limited by a number of factors. These include budget constraints, production schedules, public relations, and network sensitivity to moral issues, all of which have changed the business of telling a true story on the screen.

"At the end of the day in this market, you won't see many movies that say 'Based on a true story,' says producer Michael Jaffe, who has made over a hundred movies adapted from real events. They will say 'Inspired by real events' or 'Based on real events' or something like that because by the time you wind up compositing characters and filling in dramatic gaps, that's what you have.

Plus there are the Standards and Practices rules to adhere to and corporate policy issues dominate over all else. One network developed a true story about a union of prostitutes, but it didn't get made because the corporate policy was that they wouldn't make a movie about a prostitute who was a nice person or a hero to others. They care about their sponsors and critics who might be able to accuse or malign them in any way, shape, or form. That makes it tough to satisfy their needs and almost impossible to tell a true story any more."

Chapter Seven

CASHING IN ON CRIME

Selling Your Story

The market for true crime stories has maintained a steady appeal over time due to an innate fascination with human depravity and the forces that shape the way people act. The added elements of mystery and suspense certainly have their appeal, but the element of reality in these stories is what separates and distinguishes them from other forms of writing. In many ways, it all comes down to human nature. People cannot resist learning about the details of a crime, the motives behind the behavior of others, the way in which the criminal mind works, and the inner workings of the police and judicial systems. They love to see a complex problem solved and to have their belief in the systems society has put in place to protect them confirmed. True crime

151

stories also offer a venue for readers and viewers to explore a darker part of the world from the comfort and safety of home. Most important, the stories attract attention because they are true, and people love things that are stranger and more twisted than any fictionalized account of a crime.

But while the appeal remains, the market for the genre has changed. Part of this is the result of the cyclical nature of publishing. Trends come and go and true crime was white hot in the late 1980s and early 1990s when the nation's attention was riveted by serial killers, and both television and film projects increasingly began to emphasize "true stories." The downside of this is a current perception among publishing industry pundits that true crime has been overexposed, a belief that can be justified by citing lower sales numbers for true crime books. In fact, the market for all books is down across the board and many publishers are coming to grips with the fact that they have overpublished to their own detriment.

On the other side of the equation, the retail channels for book distribution have changed as well. The last few years have seen a significant consolidation in the bookselling industry, as huge chains have either absorbed or eliminated smaller book stores. That means that fewer books are being bought by people who pick titles out of their own interests or those of their customers. The big chains have all deployed sophisticated point-of-sale computer systems that track the turnover of individual titles and entire genres. Bookstores now stock on a six-week basis rather than the six-months-to-a-year approach of the past. Since this is designed to eliminate books that sit of the shelf, it translates into more judicious book buying on the part of retailers. This means lower sales for publishers, effectively creating a smaller overall marketplace.

But all is not lost. While some publishers have retrenched and moved away from true crime, these are typically players who jumped on the bandwagon to take advantage of the trend in the first place. Publishing houses that have always supported true crime have not backed off from their search for marketable stories and report that the area continues to be a profitable one. What has been affected has been the "big" hard-cover, true crime book, a creature whose expense and investment in terms of time and research has become increasingly harder to justify in an age of immediate media saturation. But if these books are becoming rarer, it is important to remember that there were just a handful of writers who could generate them even at the height of the market. The net result of all this is that true crime has moved solidly and profitably into the domain of the paperback bestseller.

"Paperback is the market for true crime because of the price range and the belief that much of this writing is viewed as entertainment by readers," says Charles Spicer of St. Martin's Press. "But the good news is that paperback sales are very steady in true crime. I keep hearing people say that it's collapsed because some houses have overpublished the genre, but true crime is one of our most solid markets."

What has been lost for most writers is the once-flourishing market for good true crime magazine articles. A casualty of the age of instant access in which we live and the increasingly tabloid nature of the media, the saturation coverage from television newsmagazines, print tabloids, and insta-books has made in-depth magazine articles harder to come by and even harder to sell. While modern media coverage hasn't inflicted as much damage on the demand for solidly crafted books that reveal the full story of a case, the primary problem is that most people feel as if they already know all about a crime from reading or watching the news. If a crime is particularly notorious and the coverage is extensive, many will feel overwhelmed by the attention and will even go so far as boycotting all information about a case, as they did with the O.J. Simpson trial.

Once the venue for more detailed coverage than was typically available in the daily newspaper, magazine articles have now been displaced by insta-books, which can be produced at the speed of a magazine, but offer more depth than a typical feature article. Invariably, those articles that do appear are either breathlessly sensational or more serious sections from an upcoming book. Typically, the latter have been excerpted for publicity or are the product of an established or celebrity author whose name can help market the piece. The once-popular "True Detective" series of magazines that offered a start to many writers entering the field folded some years ago. What remains is the series of low-end titles, such as *Headquarters Detective, Detective Dragnet, Startling Detective,* and others, from Globe Communications. These magazines carry on the genre's pulp tradition with stories such as "Telltale Claws of the 'Tiger Lady,'" "San Diego's Sex-Torture Bimbos," and "One-Way Ticket for the Two-Way Mistress." Despite the lurid headlines and tacky photos that adorn the covers, these magazines all offer straightforward accounts of real crimes, complete with photos, typically from the police's point of view.

What has expanded is the market for television movies and miniseries based on true crime stories. With the expansion of cable and satellite stations, there has been an explosion in the demand for "product" with which to fill the growing number of programming hours. Rough estimates from industry insiders place the demand for movies aired by major players such as CBS, NBC, ABC, Fox, Turner, Lifetime, HBO, the Family Channel, and USA at over 150 each year. Keenly aware of the attraction that true stories create in the media and the fact that there are only so many fictional books that match that level of appeal, producers are always on the lookout for a true story, especially one that offers the twists and drama of a crime case.

"The television business looks for true stories because they do better for a variety of reasons," says producer Frank von Zurnick. "If a film is based on a real person's story or a crime, then they get to do the talk show circuit, sometimes with the actor who plays them, and that's extra publicity for the show. Plus the audience hears about or sees advertisements for between a hundred twenty-five and a hundred fifty films each year and if they remember the story because it's true, it helps break through the media clutter. If they recall it, it sells it better and some of the events are so astonishing that they make great drama—especially when there's a crime involved."

In many instances, a television movie will also help drive a book's sales because the medium is limited in terms of what it can show when it comes to all the motives and the gory details. The only catch for a writer is that producers want to buy the rights to a book. If there's no book, they will simply option the story of the principals involved, say the lead detective or a prosecutor, the victim's family, and a reporter who covered the case, and turn the material over to a writer who specializes in adapting true stories to the screen. So the real bottom line for a writer works something like this: To sell a true crime story to Hollywood, you have to have a book. But to get a book, you need to sell it to a publisher. Since publishers rarely deal with unrepresented writers, that means you have to have an agent.

Finding an Agent

Every writer inevitably hears the tale of someone who sends in a manuscript to an editor who loves it and publishes it to great acclaim. Sometimes they know someone who knows the editor; sometimes it's blind luck, but the story always ends the same way—successfully. This does happen, but people also win the lottery. For every story you hear like this, there are thousands of other manuscripts that wind up in a publisher's *slush pile.* This term describes the resting place, usually a room, for the never-ending flow of unsolicited manuscripts, queries, and proposals a publisher gets.

While publishing has increasingly become a business, it is still largely a mix of art, luck, and timing because the reading public's tastes change continuously. Everybody pays attention to trends, but editors often run on instinct when a good story appears. Every book is a calculated gamble for a publisher. Therefore, the trick is getting your story onto the desk of an editor who will recommend that his or her company buy it. The upside of this scenario is that editors are always searching for a solid story put together by a good writer. The downside is that they are deluged with ideas, many of which are simply not that good, or are presented in an unprofessional manner, or are not appropriate for their company's approach to the market.

That's where having an agent comes in. Agents spend their time following the industry, attending trade shows, and meeting with editors, and can offer a direct link to a publisher who is in the market for a true crime story. They will know that while St. Martin's still publishes at least a dozen true crime books a year, HarperCollins has cut back drastically. An agent will have a more objective view of both the business and where your idea fits in the overall scheme of things than you do, and will also know how to effectively present and market a story in a way that maximizes its appeal. Always an effective match-maker, a good agent will be aware of what a certain editor is looking for and where your story is most likely to find someone interested in publishing it. Agents understand contracts and can save you both time and an endless number of headaches over the course of writing and publishing a book. Most important, they will get you a better deal.

"I went through an agent and that made a huge difference because I got twice as much as they originally offered for an advance," Scott Anderson says of his experience in selling his first true crime book. "If I had been on my own I would have never asked for that much money."

For many writers, particularly new ones, finding an agent is a daunting proposition. But the anxiety surrounding the process can be reduced by the application of common sense. It starts with research, just like the story you would like to sell. Look at one of the countless directories or writer's guides on the market. Agencies are routinely profiled in terms of their experience, expertise, and preferences. Some specialize, some do not, but all are looking for books they can sell. Listings will provide specific information and contact names and addresses that can be winnowed down into a group likely to be receptive to your work. Read trade magazines such as *Publisher's Weekly* and see who is making the deals and what publishers are looking for true crime and which agents are selling it to them.

An effective route is to network through attending conferences and workshops, or join professional associations for writers in the genre such as the American Crime Writer League (ACWL), the International Association of Crime Writers (IACW), or the Crime Writers of Canada. Some of these organizations overlap into the area of mystery or suspense fiction, as the lines between the genres can often blur when it comes to pooling resources in terms of agents or publishers who deal in crime-related stories. Everyone is usually willing to share information or provide references. Another option is to attend trade shows such as Left Coast Crime, a convention held in various cities on the West Coast since 1991, or its East Coast equivalent, the Mid-Atlantic Mystery Book Fair, or the national American Booksellers Association show that is held in Chicago each year. These events tend to attract publishers, writers, and agents in the field—many of whom share their ideas and expertise on panel discussions—and offer an opportunity to make connections.

When contacting an agent, it is essential to understand that agents guard their time carefully and routinely face the hazard of dealing with unprepared and unprofessional people. That said, a little thought and effort goes a long way in terms of making your case. Hard sells tend to be off-putting, as do cold calls and unannounced visits to an office. While there is no sure solution, the most effective place to start is with a businesslike letter introducing yourself and a strong query regarding the story you are looking for someone to represent. If you know someone who knows the agent and recommended that you make contact, be sure to mention that right up front—in a business where it is often who you know that matters most, few things work better than a connection. Also note any previous writing credits or send along a sample of your best work to show that you are not just another dreamer. Make things to the point and be as brief as possible while still covering all the bases. Remember, this is business and you have to be as businesslike and professional as possible.

Some agents will like to see an outline of a book along with the query, but rarely will they request a sample chapter the way they might with a fictionalized account. Many times a directory will list their preferences, so be sure to do a background check after you have narrowed down your list of potential agencies. There is some debate about the issue of contacting multiple agencies at once, but it is unlikely that everyone you contact will be eager to represent your work and you will probably need to cast a wide net before you get someone to respond positively. But if you do get several agents interested, be sure to be honest and direct about how you have approached the process and open about the fact that you are talking to more than one person. One word of caution: If the agent calls and asks for money, often as a "reading fee" to look at and evaluate your work, head the other way. Some agents will do this in the fiction market, but it has no place in selling nonfiction work.

"Finding an agent is always tough. I've had three and I can tell you that there's no one way to get one that has always worked," says Shannon Richardson, a former policewoman turned writer and producer, who specializes in adapting true crime stories. "The basic thing is that you have to get someone interested in your work. At one point in my career, I decided that I didn't need an agent and was on my own, but that's not the way to go. As a writer, you really do need an agent because without one you spend more time trying to get your foot in the door than you do writing and that's what you need to be doing—writing."

The Proposal

Unlike works of fiction, true crime stories are almost always sold before they are written. The sale is sometimes arranged after an extended query letter, but it is far more common to have an agent submit a detailed proposal upon which an editor can base a decision. From the writer's side, this practice allows a project to be sold

161

before it is written, saving months, perhaps even years, of potentially wasted effort. From the editor's point of view, it eliminates having to invest the time in reading through an entire draft of a book while still making it possible to determine whether or not the book will be a profitable project worth publishing.

"When I see a proposal, I'm already thinking about the jacket copy in my head. I like to think of the total package when I first get it because to sell a book you have to figure out who wants to buy it," says Mary Ann Lynch of Macmillan. "A lot of first books from major publishing houses will average a seventy-five hundred or ten thousand print run, which is in the realm of a small press, but they have such a large overhead that cuts into the promotability of the book. Positioning and getting people interested in it are key factors in bringing any book to market and you have to look at those issues right from the start."

This means that you not only have to show an editor that there is a story to be told, but that it is one that people will be willing to buy. Proposals need to sell what is different about a story, particularly where true crime is concerned. Since most people may already be familiar with a crime, or a crime that they think is just like it, the proposal has to point out what is unique. This may be a completely new revelation that was missed in the press or that came out months after the story had faded from the headlines. It might be access to a new source that you alone have cultivated—but it has to be something that an editor can see has marketing potential right from the start and it has to be clear that you can write it.

"As an editor on books like these, I'm looking for a crime that is newsworthy and a writer who has reporting credentials and/or previous book experience," explains Ballantine's Doug Grad. "Publishers are looking for a marketing angle as well as a well-written book. The angle could be the person's credentials, access to the information, or a completely new approach that no one else has come up with or can offer. This makes it tough for a newcomer because, in most cases, they don't have access or the credentials that an editor is looking for."

Most proposals are fairly short and straightforward, typically running between ten and twenty pages, although some are shorter or longer, and vary from writer to writer. But they all have the same basic elements: A title page, an introduction, a biography, a review of any competition and where the book would fit in the marketplace, a chapter-by-chapter outline, and a sample chapter or two. By the end of it, an editor should know what the crime is, who the characters are and what is compelling about them, who you are and why you are qualified to write this book, what kind of coverage has been done on the crime and whether or not there are any competing books on the market, and what makes this book different. It may sound simple, but it has to cover all these bases in a way that effectively sells the project with every sentence.

The title page is simple but important because a good title can grab attention, set the reader up for what follows, and neatly wrap up the project's overall concept. Just don't get too attached to your title because the publisher's sales and marketing departments will eventually weigh in and probably change it. The page should also carry all the essential information such as your name, your agent's name, and contact information for both of you.

The introduction section is extremely significant. As the first thing an editor will read, it has to convey the overall appeal and depth of the project while setting the stage for the rest of the proposal. It has to sell the book by proving that there is a solid idea that has a place in the market and that you are the person to do it. It should also indicate the approximate length of the book and the amount of time it will take to complete it. Mainly, it has to catch the editor's attention; the rest of the proposal won't work unless the editor keeps reading.

The biography should detail your qualifications and background. Since a true crime book is almost always sold on the merits of the story, this is somewhat less important than other sections of the proposal—but that shouldn't mean that the sales pitch stops. Areas that may be worth highlighting include public speaking or promotional abilities that can come into play after the book is published. This section is often difficult to put together because most people are reluctant to put the spotlight on their achievements or talent. But your talent is a major part of the product, so don't be shy.

The description of the competition or market coverage has to effectively convince the editor that the book will sell. If other books have been done on the case or are in progress, say so—the editor is probably aware of them anyway. If there isn't another book in the works, be sure to point out the uniqueness of the project and the overall appeal of true crime and why people would like to read it.

The bulk of the proposal should be devoted to a detailed outline of what each chapter will contain and how the material will be treated. This shows that you have carefully considered the project and have a full book's worth of material rather than an extension of a feature article. It gives the editor a clearer idea of the scope of the crime, the setting, the characters, and the degree of uncertainty involved. Each chapter should be named and concisely abstracted in a way that reads like an abbreviated version of the final manuscript but that still indicates the winding nature of the plot. Chapters have to build upon each other to tell the whole story. When you describe them, use action-oriented phrases that convey a sense of your command over the subject.

Unfortunately, with many crimes, this is much more difficult than it sounds. There may not be a conviction yet or you may have only a relatively thin collection of facts on which to base the premise of the book or there may simply be a great deal that you don't know. If this is the case, try to do as much research as you can up front and put it all in the proposal. This will help increase both the sense of depth of the circumstances surrounding the crime and the depiction of your mastery over a great deal of complicated material.

The issue of sample chapters is one that is open to debate. Many established writers dispense with them altogether. If you have done an effective job with the outline, they may simply be redundant and, since there is so much research to be done, they may be premature at best and inaccurate at worst. When in doubt, put together the first chapter because it will help set the hook for the editor. If a potential buyer gets to the end of it and wants to read more, you'll be on your way.

"I wrote up a proposal, a fairly long one of about forty-five pages, but it was difficult because there was so much I didn't know," says Scott Anderson, about his first true crime book, *The Four O'clock Murders*. "I made quite a few calls, but there was a lot that was buried or unknown because of the cult's secrecy and the geographic region it covered. It was a complicated story that spanned over thirty years with a lot of intermittent appearances by the characters, so I couldn't get it all up front, but I still managed to sell it to Doubleday."

Other things that an editor may look for in addition to a proposal may include any existing coverage of the crime, commitments from some of the principals in the case to work with you, and any photos that can be used when the book goes to press.

A proposal is a selling tool, but it is also an effective working outline for the writer. Most books don't turn out exactly as planned, but a proposal gives the writer a sense of vision and direction when sitting down at the keyboard after months of research and interviews. This can also benefit an editor who is returning to the project because it provides a window on things that have been missed or ways in which the manuscript can be improved once it is turned in.

Editors

An effective proposal will capture editors' attention and pique their interest. That can be tough when you consider the endless piles of manuscripts they have to work through, meetings and phone calls that tie them up, and the deadlines they have to meet. While there are no firm statistics, editors probably reject more than 90 percent of the proposed ideas that come their way. Some are simply bad ideas, some are redundant, but a significant percentage fail simply because they are poorly written or put together. Professionalism counts for a lot and since the proposal is the first thing editors will see from you, it will factor heavily in their estimation of your abilities and whether or not they believe that you will be able to write a book they can sell.

"True crime writing is hard work and takes a lot more time and effort than most people think. My advice to writers is always the same: Pick your crime wisely before you put together a proposal," says Kensington's Paul Dinas. "Look at it from a reader's standpoint. Is it complex and multilevel enough to merit a book? Do your homework and be ready for all the questions that I'm going to ask about motive and dates and facts and the background of the characters. Then try to line up the visuals as early as possible. Get access to the cops involved in the case, sign the family to releases. You can make all the promises in the world, but I'm looking for the thoroughness that is the cornerstone of professionalism. I want a writer who has the ability to select the relevant facts from a lot of information and is able to tell the story in a clear and dramatic way. People are going to read this book for the information it contains as well as the story. They want to see how it impacted people's lives because that is what they can relate to and I need to see that from a writer before I'll take on a book with them."

Once you get the editor interested, the process moves onto another level. Since publishing involves many factors, few of which are entirely predictable, no single person at a publishing house makes the decision to buy a book. A good proposal gets read, reread for a second opinion, and then reviewed by an editorial committee before being discussed with sales and marketing. Publishers can lose a lot of money on a book, and they want to be as secure as possible before committing to a project.

"When I get a proposal from an agent, I review it and, if I don't like it, I reject it," Doug Grad adds. "If I like it, I get a second read and we discuss the project in an editorial meeting and ask the basic questions: Is there a book here? And can the author write? It can be a great idea, but if the author can't write then that's all it is—a good idea. If all the answers are all 'yes,' then we have to ask 'is this the kind of book we want to publish?' Then there's the issue of the value-added components. 'Do we have a previously published author? Are there media contacts? Can they support the book?' This makes it hard for new or unpublished writers to break in because the publishing industry is becoming risk-averse, much like the movie industry has, because people like to see a sure bet. Then we run the numbers—how many can we sell, how large a book will it be, what will it cost to print? What's the advance? What will it cost to promote? What about the expenses of an author's tour and setting up interviews? If it all looks good, then I call the agent, make an offer, strike a deal, and then cross my fingers and hope the writer puts out a good book."

At that point, things move to the contractual stage. This is where agents can help in negotiating things like foreign or film rights, payment schedules, things that most writers never think of in the excitement of actually selling a book. Publishers often like to have as much control as possible over the long term because it offers them a greater opportunity to profit from their initial risk. But the contractual issues don't end with a publisher. One of the unique issues that true crime writers face is that of sharing revenues with some of their sources in exchange for new or exclusive material. One of the downsides of living in a tabloid age is that many people have come to feel that they can get rich off the misfortune that has befallen them or their families. Urban legends abound of people who have made it by selling their story for millions to the highest bidder and this is an attitude that true crime writers are encountering with increasing frequency. But if there is a uniform word of advice on this subject, it is simple: Don't.

"I make it a point to never share book revenues with a source such as a detective," says Jay Fletcher. "I always do it at the film level. In one case I offered 20 percent of movie rights—not book rights—because that's where the money is and it gets factored into the price on top of what you can get for the rights to the book." Regarding rights, she says, "I would caution every true crime writer not to sell your broadcast rights to the publisher. They are book people and that's what they're buying—the book, not all the other rights to your talent. That's not their business."

With the contract in hand, many writers think that "all" they have left to do is write the book. As challenging as that task is, it is far from the end of the road. Once a manuscript is turned in, an editor will probably ask for revisions and may make structural changes to the story. The relationship between an editor and writer can vary widely depending on the personalities, approaches, and skills involved. Some editors are hands-on and very detail oriented, just as some writers like to share their work on a chapter-by-chapter basis while others will hoard away everything until the due date and then deliver an entire manuscript. In every case, facts will have to be checked, a legal read will be done by the publisher's lawyers, and then the marketing begins to drive sales as the publication date approaches. This is where editors are looking for a writer who can add "something else" to a book's appeal, something that will make it sell once it hits the shelves.

"I like people who are savvy—people who are willing to be part of the promotional campaign as well," says Mary Ann Lynch. "That doesn't stop once the manuscript is finished. Look at John Grisham. His first book didn't sell, so he went to bookstores and signed them himself. Tamara Janowitz hawked her book on the streets of New York. People have to be willing to go along with the publisher's needs and they have to be creative as well."

This is a responsibility that some writers understand better than others. One of the most successful of all true crime writers, Ann Rule, has created a virtual mini-industry through her effective approach to marketing her talent. A frequent lecturer and panelist when she's not touring in support of a new project, she also publishes her own newsletter as a means of answering fan mail from readers. Keenly aware of the growing reach of the Internet, she has added regular appearances on interactive forums such as America OnLine's BookPage. While no one would deny the popularity of Rule's prolific output, she isn't shy about doing what it takes to make her books move.

"I started out small, signing books locally in places like the Safeway, drugstores, at annual picnics, and then meeting with writers' groups of five or more," Rule says of her approach to marketing her work. "You have to be accessible and be out there, signing books, talking to people, and doing whatever it takes to sell those copies. When I went on the promotional tour for the *Stranger Beside Me,* I went to forty cities and lost twenty-five pounds. There were no media assistants at the time and I was always lost, but you have to start at the bottom, get out there, get people to know you, and always be accessible."

Hollywood and True Crime

Over the course of the 1990s, the television and movie industries have increasingly gravitated toward "reality-based programming," a programming term for stories based on real-life events. This approach was popular in television because it reduced production costs and seemed to hit a nerve with viewers. Movie executives liked it because some form of the disclaimer "based on real events" helped a film in marketing and advertising campaigns. The people upon whose lives the productions were based often did the talk show circuit with the star that represented them, and magazines like *People* and *US* were quick to publicize the "story behind the movie"— all of which equaled free and extensive publicity in the eyes of a network or studio.

True crime stories have had a place in Hollywood ever since the adaptation of Capote's *In Cold Blood* proved popular at the box office. But over the last few years, the trend has been toward adapting existing or original stories for network movies of the week or the occasional miniseries. If the case is in the news, particularly if it is one that has garnered national attention, it is likely that several independent producers are not far behind the reporter who broke the case. These people will try to sign up the rights of several of the principals and often the story of the reporter who is covering the case or who might have signed a deal to do an insta-book. With the rights in hand, they will set about adapting the combined stories in a way that suits a dramatic format.

Producers are voracious readers and they devour everything with print on it at an astonishing rate in the search for new material. Books are extremely popular because they solve several problems from the producer's point of view. The first is that they consolidate the issue of rights. Legal exposure is a major issue in television and the legal departments of both the independent producer and the networks often have the final say on a script. By buying the rights from an author, they often save the money they would have spent trying to sign up several people for an original adaptation. The second is that books have an emotional currency in a highly risk-averse industry. After all, there is no science to making a good or popular movie and the fact that someone else has already taken a calculated gamble on the project is highly appealing. Plus all the research is done and the basic plot points have been developed.

Selling a book to the movies typically happens in two steps. The first is the option where a producer buys the rights to a book from an author. This gives the producer the opportunity to turn around and try and sell the project to the studios or a network for a specific period or time. Most options are for a year and have a renewal clause built into them. Depending on the success of the book or the author's track record or name recognition, the option money could be small or substantial, but it is usually not as big as people think it is. In fact, in many cases there is no money exchanged at all, just the promise of payment if the project is sold. It is not uncommon for projects to be optioned a number of times before they actually get sold—and even then there is no guarantee that the movie will ever be made.

"I've been pretty successful in having my projects optioned for adaptations. I'll negotiate an option on a book for a year, with a year renewal. I have set fees: X amount for a miniseries, another for a movie of the week, and another for a feature film," says Fred Rosen, who has sold a number of his books to the movies. "I also try to attach myself as a creative consultant so I'll have some input on the outcome of the product and I get a fee for that. It's important to understand that it's all

Monopoly money in the movie business. Hollywood people always throw big figures around, but who cares? The fact is 90 percent of the things that are optioned don't get made. So it's just a game, but the game ends when it gets a green light and goes into production. Writers can get taken in by all those zeroes in a figure really easy, but I've found that you can't take it too seriously."

Rosen's perspective is interesting because he comes from a film background; he lived in Los Angeles for a number of years and has an understanding of the way the business works that most writers don't share. In many respects, Hollywood is a place of conflicting images and reality. People seem to dress more casually, but they are often far more serious than someone from Wall Street when it comes down to negotiating a deal. Big numbers float in the air when projects are being discussed, but the budget for a two-hour television movie can often be smaller than what a major feature will spend on a single special effect. If this sounds confusing, it pales when compared to some of the creativity employed in contract-writing and bookkeeping practices. That's why it is essential to have someone representing you when Hollywood comes knocking. Unfortunately, the literary agent you have worked so hard to get may not be the best person to protect you.

"If possible, try and develop a relationship with an agent in Hollywood. A good place to start is to ask your literary agent to introduce you to the agent they use out there," says Lowell Cauffiel. "Don't get me wrong, New York agents are very good at what they do, but I've noticed that the film people don't go to work until about three o'clock in the afternoon and most literary agents are on the train headed home at that point in the day. The result is that a lot of stuff falls through the cracks. The average attention span of the average producer is one day, so you can't get what you need from your guy in New York no matter how good they are. You really need someone in Los Angeles because you need two agents to play both fields."

Once the work gets sold, it has to get made. This can be a harrowing experience filled with emotional ups and downs because there is little logic to what actually makes it into production and what doesn't. Most true crime writers take their fee and start on another book project and hope for the best. But when a book does get the green light from a network, new problems arise as the process of adapting reality to a three- or seven-act dramatic framework begins. While the essence of the story remains the same, the approach in telling it undergoes a radical—and to the original writer, often unrecognizable—transformation.

As producer Janet Faust-Krusi pointed out in Chapter 5, few real-life characters live at a pace that is well adapted to the screen. You have to compress days or years into an hour or two while remaining true to the dynamics of the story, and that means that a lot of what the book writer and the original characters regard as "the facts" must disappear from the new production.

Many writers try to have some input in this process by contractually attaching themselves to a production as creative or script consultants. This is common and, in fact, encouraged by many of the producers who option stories for adaptation. The reasoning behind it is that the writer is a one-stop reference guide for any real issues of dispute. But what many writers fail to realize is that the process of adapting a book into a script is one that keeps the relationship between the basic elements of the story intact while compressing or compositing everything and everyone else to fit within the prescribed format of the medium. The result is that the original writer may have very little input in what the final product looks like.

"I was a script consultant but they didn't pay much attention to me," Harry MacLean says of his experience. "I would review the script and do twenty pages of notes and they'd ignore it. Then I'd get the rewritten script back and the same thing would happen again. It was a lot of small detail, but they're not interested in that—things like they don't have dirt roads, they're all gravel in that part of the state; or whether or not a guy would wear a leather jacket. That's when I realized they didn't care, that they were writing something else and that was a more lasting reality."

Other writers will negotiate a deal that makes them the writer who does the adaptation, but this is far less common than you might think. Producers deal with the problems inherent in adapting a story from one medium to another all the time and usually have a corps of writers who specialize in this. Furthermore, the process of adapting true stories is specialized enough so that there is a relative handful of production companies involved in it. The people who run these companies are keenly aware of where the problems are and would rather pay someone who is an expert at solving them than ride the learning curve with someone who means well, particularly if the production schedule or budget is tight. Then there is the issue of the emotional attachment a writer has to a long and complex work.

"Part of the problem is that a writer produces a 'child' when they write a book. They often have three years into the thing and its very hard to let go and see it go into another medium," says producer Frank von Zurnick. "Actors address things differently, the pace is different, the director has nuances that change the way things come across and that's different for writers. They see it as what it was and the change is sometimes difficult to accept, particularly for journalists and sometimes even for novelists. They see it one way and it comes out another. I also won't deny that there are people in my field who are more sensationalistic than we are in their approach, and that has an impact on the way some things come out."

In the end, the writer will have little say on what or how the final project appears on the screen. On the whole, most producers who specialize in adapting true crime are as committed to maintaining the integrity of the story as the original writer is in a book. They are skilled storytellers, but they work in a medium that has different needs and one set of skills doesn't always translate neatly into the other. Some writers realize this from the start and move on to the next proposal while others learn these lessons from painful experience.

"All of my books have been optioned as films, but not all of them have been made," says Darcy O'Brien, "although the NBC movie of the week based on *The Hillside Strangler* got a twenty-three rating and was reshown a lot and that helped book sales. That was not a terribly unpleasant experience. But some of the adapted scripts are so horrible that you're glad they never made the thing. A lot of it has to do with who picks up the project. Some screenwriters can be asinine and have contempt for the material because it's 'just a job' and it shows in the writing. Others are deeply committed and want to do the best work possible. I had never been interested in doing my own adaptations, but I did try doing it once just to see what it was like. It was an agonizing experience and I realized right away that it was not my medium. It was like everything I had learned and struggled to achieve as a prose writer was worth nothing because the dialogue is completely different. There is an unreal sense of time with a narrative and film is real

179

time. You have a simple equation: One minute equals half a page and you're bound by that. There were also network executives interfering and they were changing the motivation of the characters because they thought it was too dark even though it was based on real people. It was incredibly frustrating and I finally gave up trying to do it."

Chapter Eight

TRUE CRIME WRITERS CONFESS

On the Record

If the presence of certain elements help to define the genre—a horrible murder, compelling characters, twisted motives, and a stranger-than-truth plot—the opposite is true of the people who write the stories. True crime writers come from all sorts of backgrounds. The field is filled with former journalists, lawyers, cops, novelists, and screenwriters who have come to true crime by commitment, chance, or coincidence. Some are relentlessly commercial in their approach; others are more committed to the essence of telling a compelling tale in a way that helps illuminate a darker part of the world we live in. But in every case, these are people who are bound by a commitment to honesty, accuracy, and running down every lead no matter how long it takes.

181

Given the level of research and the serpentine nature of many of the stories, one thing is certain: True crime writing is not for the impatient or the undetermined. It is not uncommon for a writer to spend between two and three years—and in some cases as many as seven—putting the pieces of a story together before it will even reach an editor's desk. There are the emotional ups and downs of tracking a subject that is often shrouded in shame and long-hidden secrets held by reluctant witnesses or families who would rather forget. Competition from other writers and well-heeled media outlets has changed the range and scope of cases that can be successfully covered and the cyclical nature of publishing-industry trends has altered the genre's packaging and position in the marketplace.

Despite these challenges, true crime writers are an unusually dedicated lot. They are as fascinated as their readers by the fact that no two cases are ever the same, and their work always manages to reveal some greater truth about the time, place, and society in which we live. But how do they do it? How do they find cases, get people to talk, face down psychotic killers and crabby cops, and put together the pieces of shattered lives in a way that rivets a reader's attention? What does it take to sell a book or a screenplay or to adapt years of work into a sixty-minute drama built around commercial breaks?

Since there is no substitute for experience, the profiles that follow offer direct insights into the talents and techniques you will need to succeed in true crime writing.

Drawn from an extensive series of in-depth interviews with the people who have come to dominate every aspect of the genre, these profiles provide real-world advice, sharpened by years of success. Told in each writer's own words, these are the stories behind the stories.

Scott Anderson

A longtime journalist, Anderson began his career as a war correspondent. His books include *War Zones: Voices from the World's Killing Grounds, Inside the League,* and *The Four O'clock Murders.* He has investigated the Russian Mafia and racketeers operating in Northern Ireland as contributing editor to *Harpers* magazine, and his work has appeared in the *New York Times Magazine, The Nation, Outside,* the *Boston Globe,* and the *Cleveland Plain Dealer.* His first novel, *Triage,* will be published by Scribners in the fall of 1998, and a nonfiction book, *Bad Places,* will be published by Doubleday in 1999.

* * * * *

"In 1988, four people were murdered in three different locations in Texas in broad daylight and the story went national because of the unusual nature of it. I read about them in a small blurb in the newspaper and I recognized the names of the victims from a book I had read years earlier on a cult operating down there. It struck me because the names were unusual, Welsh, and they stuck in my mind. I started calling around to reporters on the *Houston Post* and the Dallas papers and they brought me up to date on a lot of bizarre stuff that had happened since the book was done ten years before. That's when I started to think that there might be a story, because I found that at least twenty people had been killed that the cops knew about and the cult had a death list that they were working their way through. The killers knew that if they killed one, the others would disappear so they decided to do them all at once. All the murders happened at 4 P.M., all the killers wore matching disguises and drove stolen black pickups, and all the witness descriptions matched. This left the police unable to convict because they couldn't tell any of the suspects apart. I was fascinated by the complexity of the story because it really was about the question of where madness and religion meet, that what can look like complete craziness to one person can look like signs of godliness to another. But one of the big challenges of the book was that the suspects, the cops, and the cult were spread all across the western half of the U.S.

"I wrote up a proposal, a fairly long one of about forty-five pages, but it was difficult because there was so much I didn't know. I made quite a few calls, but there was a lot that was buried or unknown because of the cult's secrecy and the geographic region it covered. It was a complicated story that spanned over thirty years with a lot of intermittent appearances by the characters, so I couldn't get it all up front, but I still managed to sell it to Doubleday. I went through an agent and that made a huge difference because I got twice as much as they originally offered for an advance. If I had been on my own I would have never asked for that much money.

"If I was going to offer advice on doing a true crime book, I'd say choose your story carefully. There's always a first enthusiasm for a story, but you really have to think on it for a few days or even a few weeks. You have to ask yourself 'Do I really want to give up two to three years of my life to this story?' because when push comes to shove, you will have to live with both the story and that decision. Another thing to consider is the amount of attention a case is getting. While this one got some attention, it was too complex for the national media to follow through on. You don't want to compete with the media on a big case because everyone's got a lawyer, the cops are much more tight-lipped, everyone wants to get paid, and you know that there's three or four other writers who can scoop you out. That's a lot of pressure. You also want to avoid stories that are unfolding because you will get frozen out. National stories have a glare to them that makes them difficult to crack unless you have a lot of money and resources, otherwise you can't compete. The more uncertain the outcome of a story is, the more frustrated you will be. There's also the issue of resolution. Most editors like a case that's wrapped up, but when a story is winding through the court systems everyone has lawyers and they are harder to get to in terms of access.

So you really need to have some sort of resolution occur before you can get a lot of information. You can follow a story while it's unfolding, but it can take forever because there are motions, pretrial hearings, discovery, and appeals and you won't get the really good stuff until it's over and people are willing to talk. But even then, I've found that there's a difference between a book and an article in the way people deal with you. A book is in the future somewhere and people are much more forthcoming because they're not worried about seeing their words come back at them in week or a month to haunt them. They're just a lot more accessible.

"Two of the big skills a true crime writer needs to have is to be able to fit into the local scene and to be as nonjudgmental as possible when dealing with local people. I found that I have to be chameleon-like, changing between the appearance of a clean-living Mormon boy to cult members and a hard-bitten journalist to the cops. But if you let them, people will tell you the most amazing things about themselves. The big thing is having the ability to listen—which, unfortunately, a lot of reporters don't do very well. If you listen closely you can hear a change in their language or see a shift in their body language that's revealing something else. You're almost like a psychiatrist, gently circling back to the subject, to what went on, to what they're holding back. I never take notes when I'm interviewing someone unless it's a cop. I always tape conversations with a small recorder that I put out of the way, out of the sight line. I always keep the subject as vague as possible and let people talk. It takes a lot of time, but it's really the only way that you can get sensitive material. With the Russians, I needed to hang out and drink for eight hours a day just to get ten to twenty-five minutes of useful material. That's a little different because you can't be direct with any Mafia type and anything to do with them is a huge investment of time. They deal with informants who try to infiltrate them all the time and there's a real hierarchy to the organization. You gradually learn small secrets and if those secrets don't come back to them, then they trust you more and more. I spent seven years hanging out with the IRA guys who were operating protection rackets before I could write the story.

"By the time you sit down to write, you've got to have your research organized and prioritized. I've found that secondary sources can vary in importance. I've gone through fifteen file drawers of records on a book, all of which helps build the overall story but doesn't make it come to life. What I found interesting and helpful were the police reports because you can see where and when they learn what. It helps create a timeline by looking at the way the investigation unfolded and then using that to help create the arc of the story. It's really important to choose a focus and then stay with it because you're going to have too much information if you've done your research right. But your viewpoint depends on the scope and complexity of the story. Sometimes the more complex ones have to be less creative and more straightforward to avoid confusing the reader. In the Texas book, I did a lot through dialogue because all the murders took place over a forty-year span and there were so many characters involved. That was something I had to solve through a structural approach because it would have overwhelmed the reader. But dialogue can be tricky too. I don't like re-created conversations when I'm the reader and I think it is a slippery slope for a writer because it calls into question the veracity of the story you are telling. I always try to get several sources on any conversation and have found that police interrogation records often contain elements of conversations that can be useful."

Edna Buchanan

A Pulitzer Prize-winning reporter who made her name in the bloody streets of southern Florida, Buchanan covered more than three thousand murders in sixteen years of writing for the *Miami Herald*. Yet rather than hardening her, the process of continually confronting extreme violence raised her empathy for the untold stories of the deceased. She made the transition to writing true crime while still a reporter, and the success of her books eventually led to her leaving journalism altogether. Buchanan's nonfiction titles include *Five Years of Rape and*

Murder, The Corpse Had a Familiar Face, Never Let Them See You Cry, and *Byline: Edna Buchanan*—among many others. Her work has been adapted for television movies and Buchanan has used her success in creative nonfiction to fulfill her lifelong ambition of writing crime-driven fiction.

* * * * *

"I didn't have a college education or even know anything about journalism when I started writing. But I've always been addicted to stories ever since my mom read to me as a child. At age four I told everyone that I would write books one day because I loved stories and always wanted to know the endings. So after high school, I got a job on a small paper where I did a bit of everything, celebrity interviews, police news, health stories—you name it. Then I got to the *Herald* and was a general assignment reporter. I did a few police stories as part of that assignment and then moved onto the criminal court beat. I came across a lot of newsworthy cases, but when I went back to the *Herald*'s library I would discover that there was no initial coverage of the crime. I spent a year doing that and just before I was supposed to go back on general assignment I told my editor that someone really ought to go to make a beat out of this. Nothing fancy, just a police beat where you'd go to the stations to talk to people on a regular basis, visit the morgue to see what came in overnight, and track cases right from the start.

Essentially, it would be covering crime right in the streets. I suggested it to my editor and he said 'Good idea. Do it.' I never volunteered or even thought it should be me, but there I went, right into the streets.

"I covered five thousand violent deaths, three thousand of which were homicides, over the next sixteen years. I was the first woman reporter who had done this and I would go to every homicide scene called in. It was strange at first, but the cops grew accustomed to seeing me there and I became like a piece of furniture on the scene, just part of the background. In 1981, Miami had six hundred thirty-seven murders and broke all records. I covered every single one. My editors only wanted me to cover the major murder of the day, but I felt every murder was major, at least to the victims and their families. The *Herald* was the city's newspaper of record and I wanted to tell everyone's story. It was a nightmare year because I was always going from murder scene to murder scene and then trying to find a way to get everyone's story in the paper. Sometimes I would do it as a 'trend' story and put four murders in a single lead, or I might devote a paragraph to each case in a 'murder roundup' type of piece. But I did it because I felt a moral obligation and a sense of justice within me. Justice is so rare and elusive in our society and a reporter can be a victim's best friend because they are among the few people left in the world who can make things happen. If you write a story about injustice, things can happen as a result. But many editors think that there are a lot of murders that aren't worth covering, bar shootings or whatever, but there's always a story. There's always something there if you scratch hard enough. A lot of writers think that there are things that aren't worth writing about, but a killing has an impact on everyone around the victim, on every life it touches. Then there are the dynamics of how it brought all these people to a place in space and time for it to have happened. There's always something there that's revealing about people and society. I really believe that every story is different, even the ones that appear to be the same, because you can find incredible twists and turns and irony in every case.

"One of the cases I covered was on missing persons. I did a Sunday magazine piece about the 'most intriguing missing persons in Dade County.' In my research I found a case about two missing eleven-year-old boys who were friends. They had gone to one of their after-school jobs to pick up a paycheck and just disappeared; they never got the check or were seen by the kids' boss and had been missing four years. Then I got a call saying that the cops had arrested a rapist caught in the act and he started confessing to all these murders once he was in custody. He had killed four people and buried their bodies all over the country. I put two and two together and realized that the two boys he mentioned were the two kids in the file sitting on my desk. He had kidnapped, raped, and tortured them, and then buried them in

Mississippi. When the cops came back from retrieving the bodies, they said I ought to talk to this guy, that I'd like him. I wouldn't go to interview him, but he started writing me, saying that he liked my writing and that I was the only one who was accurate. At the same time, a publisher saw my stories in the *Herald* and approached me to do a true crime book on this case. It took three years and was a nightmare, but it was fascinating. The killer had a photographic memory, and I spent a hundred twenty-five hours in a cell with him. I never felt frightened because he wanted me to tell the story with accuracy. It was like a deathbed confession because he thought he would get the death penalty. He also didn't like the status a rapist had in prison, so he confessed to being a serial killer to elevate his rank with other inmates. Then the cops took him out to dinner, brought him cigarettes, took him on trips to dig up the bodies, and that beat sitting in jail all day. But a woman judge sentenced him to three hundred sixty-five years instead of death and then he didn't want the story told. The book was published as *Five Years of Rape and Murder* and I still get calls from people who have a copy of it or are doing a paper on serial killers. Robert Ressler, the FBI expert on profiling serial killers, used to use it as a textbook in his classes at Quantico. That led to two more books, but they were mostly about covering murders in Miami. Still, I learned that a good case to write about has a survivor or a victim that the reader can identify with. After that, people are looking for sex, crime, and tragedy.

"Many years ago, an editor told me to stay off the police beat because it makes you callused to things, but I don't think you can grow calluses on your heart. If anything, it made me far more sensitive to the plight of people. Many times they're wronged twice—the killing first, and then the system will let them down. That's what most people don't understand, that if there is an arrest, which is rare, there will be deposition after deposition and hearing after hearing. Then, if there should be a conviction, of which there are very few, there are appeals, time off for good behavior, work release programs, and it's never over for the victim's family. Never. There's never any closure for them. There are plenty of cases where I know who did the murder, the cops know, the victim's family knows, but the prosecutor's office won't file charges because they don't have enough evidence. That's why true crime is deceiving as a genre, because most cases don't get solved. Prosecutors are very aware of their conviction rates and they like a sealed case with a smoking gun *and* a signed confession. How often does that happen? So a lot of cases just never get prosecuted and the murderer walks free because smart criminals don't leave smoking guns or sign confessions. People like to think the system works and they often look to true crime to reassure them, but it really doesn't. Things fall through the cracks or are pushed off a desk and then replaced by the crime that happens next week. Plus cops have a short life span. They last twenty years at most and they get moved around from assignment to assignment and things just fall by the wayside and go unsolved. It's disappointing but true.

"That's one of the reasons I've switched to fiction. I love the change because when you're a journalist there's so many stories that don't have endings. There's unsolved murders, missing people are never found, unidentified corpses come and go, and you're always asking 'Who are these people? Doesn't someone miss them?' In fiction, it's an absolute joy because you can wrap up all the loose ends every time. But true crime can be much wilder than fiction because you couldn't make some of that stuff up. In either case, I believe that if you're a storyteller at heart, you know how best to tell a story. The beginnings are the most important because we live in an age where attention spans are very short, so you have to get up front. A lot of times, I'll tell the story to a friend or a neighbor and then, just by hearing it out loud, I'd be able to get the lead. Or it will come to me while I'm driving or in the shower or wherever. The lead is really important and the first line is always the most important thing. It should be both provocative and informational. You have to be fair with the readers and not try to grab them with some line that is there for some sort of sensationalism, but you always have to keep them reading. I always like to have sharp leads, because as a reporter I found that so many readers never followed the jump of a story to the back pages. So I learned to make a point to write the stories in a way where you have to go along with the flow early in my career. It seems to have worked."

Lowell Cauffiel

A former staff writer for the *Detroit News* Sunday magazine, Cauffiel won awards for his crime stories four years in a row. Although relatively short at five thousand words each, they were unusual, in-depth pieces that looked behind the case and beyond the standard "who, what, when, where, and how" of traditional newspaper journalism. Cauffiel also freelanced for *Rolling Stone* magazine and was familiar with the New Journalism approach to nonfiction. Influenced by true crime writers such as Hugh Aynsworth, Steve Michaud, and Jack Olsen, he began applying fiction techniques such as symbolism, metaphor, and rising conflict in his nonfiction. Well known for his thorough research, he has focused on cases in his native Midwest and has produced a number of hardcover books. Of these, *Masquerade* and *Eye of the Beholder* are the best known. His most recent title is *House of Secrets*. Cauffiel has also had several books optioned by film companies and has worked as a consultant on true crime scripts.

* * * * *

"I think all true crime books are really morality tales and that's what people look for when they read one. To the readers, the true crime story offers a character check for themselves because they want to know what made these people commit these acts. These books allow them to explore a natural fear in themselves. Deep inside they're afraid that they may one day commit a crime or a murder and they want to know what makes them different from these people. As a writer, my goal is to really disturb the readers—to access their emotions, to tell a story that brings these feelings out. My books take readers to a place they cannot normally get to and the stories reveal not only the motives and actions of the key participants, but also a bigger theme that is part of the American experience. They also tend to emphasize people who appear to be one thing, but are really something completely different underneath. That's what drove me to write *Masquerade*. Although he appeared to be someone who was normal, the main character was obsessed and in the grip of dark forces. I wanted to know what made people want to destroy themselves, why they go over the edge. I had been close enough to those things myself, but I lived and went on. I found that it boiled down to choices, the choices people make are what determine their destiny. That's what these books are about—the choices people make and the impact of those decisions on their lives and the lives of others. That's something that people can relate to and the number one person in my mind is the reader. The reader has to be able to identify with these characters because as you 'peel the onion' of their personality throughout the book, the contrast between the horror inside and their outward appearance is that much more powerful.

"But to do that you have to do as much research as possible. On each of my books I do a minimum of three hundred hours of taped interviews and try to find everything about a person, all the details that makes them like us and not like us. This includes how they dress, what they eat, their family situation, what they drive, their basic likes and dislikes, everything I can come across. It's the only way that you can uncover that dichotomy of what people appear to be and what they really are. As a rule, I stick to cases in the Midwest, usually within driving distance, because if it isn't close by, expenses can eat up your advance in travel, food, and phone costs. I try to schedule tasks when I'm researching a book, but once you open up a thread it can take days to run it down. It's a simple fact that the quality of your true crime book will be directly proportional to the quality of your research. Typically, I talk to somewhere between two hundred fifty and five hundred people on a project and my last book was the result of nine to ten shelf-feet of documentation covering everything from court transcripts and police reports to weather reports and psychological profiles. I collect everything when I'm researching and it's amazing what turns up—phone bills, birth certificates, letters between family members, pictures, a lot of stuff that's often seized with a search warrant. It all starts you off on other leads.

"The trial transcript is a good starting point that gives you the cast of characters and a list of who you will need to talk to when researching. It's also a big part of your legal protection because anything that's said on the witness stand is fair game. This is especially important in sexual matters because it establishes the parameters of what you can write about without fear of lawsuits. Even then, I check everything from brand names of things to weather reports of the time and place of events. If I get an allegation, I try to get multiple sources but I try to stay away from attribution. If I can confirm that something was said, the legal standard is 'a reasonable facsimile thereof' when recreating dialogue. But I try to go one step further. I spend so much time with these people and I tape them, trying to get their exact words and tone. Then I will run the section back by the other person and see if they agree with it. One of my rules is that I won't go with one person's unconfirmed version of what was said in a conversation unless the other person is dead.

"But you've also got to be able get access and get people to talk to you. You can't appear to be too interested at first and you have to be patient. I always make people feel that I am like them, rather than different from them. I will use old newspaper tricks like send flowers to people who turn me down and thank them. I never tell anyone that I want to interview them because that allows them to turn you down before they meet you. I just say that I want to come over and introduce myself and explain what I am doing. That I'm doing this book and you'll be in it and I'd like to tell you about it, whether or not you want to be involved is up to you. I always set a meeting in a neutral place and never bring a tape or a notebook. Instead, I give them a published book, tell them about my philosophy, and tell them what I'm going to do and then say I think it would be helpful to participate. That gets 80 percent of the people involved on board. The other 20 percent get the choice of sitting down with me for an in-depth interview and being assigned a pseudonym. If they don't, I explain that I will be forced to use their name and what I have in the public record, which may be incomplete information that will present an inaccurate portrayal of them.

"I have a good idea where I'm going when I start to write. The first third of the book is the toughest and I can often spend five months getting the initial chapters right. Right up front I write a section in a way that implies all sorts of things, usually through a scene that encapsulates the book like a giant thesis statement and hints at what's to come. I like to build to the crime. Everything I put in has to reinforce the plot, every detail must advance the plot, and that's a mistake a lot of budding nonfiction writers make, not understanding how to use details appropriately. I always develop my characters throughout the entire book and they aren't fully revealed

199

until the final pages. A tendency among many writers is to front-load the book with an entire chapter about someone's past and then move on to someone or something else; that just spends the capital up front. Part of the suspense, mystery, and appeal of true crime writing is the ability to hook the readers and compel them to read all the way through to the end. It's much more effective that way. I love when people tell me they read the last chapter first and didn't get anything from it. That means I'm doing it right."

Jay Fletcher

As the very first female police officer hired by the city of Chicago, Jay Fletcher knows all about tough assignments. Faced with departmental policies that restricted her advancement, she filed a federal lawsuit with eleven other women over the right to open the full spectrum of police positions to female employees in 1973. After winning this landmark case, she spent six years on patrol before moving into the department's News Affairs office where she acted as the main liaison between the police department and the city's notoriously raucous press corps. As part of her training, Fletcher attended the FBI Academy for advanced courses in press and news media relations. She began contributing true crime stories to several magazines in the 1980s before writing her first book, *Deadly Thrills*. This led to her second book, *A Per-*

fect Gentleman, which sold well and was bought by NBC as a movie of the week. Recently retired from the police force, Fletcher is currently working on two new books.

* * * * *

"I had no formal training as a writer until I began working in press relations for the department, but that was quite an experience. The police department is a natural attraction for the media because any time you have a person in a uniform with a gun, you have the potential for controversy. It often becomes a target for the press when ratings are low or other news is scarce. But it was extremely valuable because I got to see how both sides worked. I wrote lots of pieces for the superintendent's office, press releases, articles, and so forth, as well as op-ed pieces for the *Chicago Tribune*. Due to the way things were structured politically, most of these went out under someone else's name, but that's when my writing really began to take off.

"Like many people, I had always written for myself, but once I saw my articles get published I realized that I could do it on my own. So I bought a *Writer's Market* and read it cover to cover. Young, cocky, and arrogant, I picked the national magazines that paid the best and began sending out queries. I got rejected quickly and consistently and that made me reconsider my approach. I thought, 'Well, what can I do that would make sense?' Then I saw *Official Detective Magazine*. I got their writer's guidelines and started turning local and regional cases into articles. I got $250 a story, plus $12 for each photograph. The first one took me three months to write, the second ten days, and the rest a single night each. I did over a hundred stories for them and it was good steady work because I had a formula that was effective. Best of all, I was collecting checks for what I was doing. I also started writing for the *National Centurion*, a magazine written by police about police. It was very slick, very nice, and I did cover stories for them on all sorts of things—gypsy crime in America, underwater scuba units, whatever came along.

"Then I came across the story of Robin Gecht at work. He would take his three teenage followers and they would kidnap women, take them to a remote spot, cut off their breasts, eat them, murder them, and then hold sacrifices with the remaining body parts. This attracted huge attention from the national media and I had to be the instant expert on the investigation as part of my job. So I called the detectives, got all the records, and immersed myself, and then began to hold forth as the spokeswoman on how the case was progressing. But it stayed with me and haunted me. When it came to trial several years later, I wrote a double-length feature—twelve thousand words—called the 'Chicago Ripper' for *Official Detective*. It really affected me because of the victims involved, I really identified with them. All of the other cases I wrote about I promptly forgot, but I just couldn't get this one out of my head.

Finally, I just decided to write a book on it because I couldn't answer several questions. Gecht was never tried for murder even though he got the longest attempted murder sentence ever handed down. But why didn't we get him on murder? I couldn't answer that. I also wanted to know what he did to motivate those teenagers to do that with him. Did he get them to follow him because they all had the same hunger inside and they all recognized each other on a deep level, or were they just normal and dumb kids that he somehow 'flipped'? It was the psychological underpinnings of it.

"Once I decided to write a book, I asked the publisher of *Official Detective* if she knew any agents. I didn't know anything about writing books, so I went to the library and read every book on writing books and immersed myself in it. I used a contact I had with a local news affiliate who connected me to an agent and I sent off a query letter and a proposal for what became *Deadly Thrills*. The agent took it to a big publishing house and they loved it. I was a strong female type—a career police officer, that sort of thing—and they wanted to set me up as the 'new Ann Rule.' But I had some personal problems and I put the book off until the last minute and did a lousy job. The publisher rejected it and I took some time, straightened things out in my life, and wound up rewriting it over the course of two months. It did very well.

"Two months later, I was in Houston visiting friends and heard about a story down there about a local young police officer getting killed by a serial killer. He was the only police officer killed in the town of Beaumont since 1928, so you can imagine the reaction. I knew an FBI agent in the area and he gave me information about the case. It turned out that Michael Lee Lockhart was a killer who had left a trail of young women in his path and wound up being sentenced to death in three states. He was an amazing con artist, very smooth, and I wound up spending a lot of time with him on death row. With all of the material in hand I started writing *A Perfect Gentleman*. I had dropped my agent from the first book by then and I went to the booksellers convention in Chicago where I met Paul Dinas from Kensington and pitched it to him. He told me to send a proposal to him and two weeks later he called me back and said if he could have the book by November he would take it. It was June and I was working full time, but I did it. I would come home, let out the dog, change my clothes, sit down, and write until midnight every day. It sold out first print run and NBC bought the rights for a movie of the week.

"Having written both articles and books, I can tell you that there has to be a lot of supporting interest and material to make a book work. Something has to set this whole series of people and events apart from the twenty others that are reported in the paper every week. All the surrounding circumstances have to be interesting because the crime itself is only a thumbtack that holds the big picture to the bulletin board. I don't have a set of criteria about what I'd like to work on, so I listen to everybody tell me about everything. But when a spark hits, it's sort of like the weird attraction that happens between people. You get the feeling that 'Hmm, that's one I'd like to know better.' There's a strange sort of magnetism that happens between a writer and the story that's hard to explain, but it's a feeling every writer knows.

"I didn't have a direct source on my first book and I struggled with every piece of information in it. Now I won't do a book unless I have a solid source, either the criminal, or a cop, or a family member. I've sniffed after many stories that didn't fly, because you have to look at a lot of them. Since I'm a former cop, I usually start with the detective and then have them get in touch with the family and make an introduction. But the cops have become far more astute in this regard because they realize they have a potential pot of gold here and I walk a fine line in getting their help. I dislike this part of the process, flattering the detective enough to make him or her want to help me, but not so much that they want to think that they are sitting on a pile of cash. On my first contact, I state my credentials and then say I'm a writer and that I'm 'interested' in the case. I always tone down my natural enthusiasm for the story and try and get them to help me. They will start with talking about the crime endlessly because they think that's what the book is all about. But it's not—it's really about everything else surrounding it—and I already know about the crime. After they get done, I say 'Okay, now tell me about the family.' In every case, they say 'The family loves me.' That's because he's the only guy who looks like he's trying to give them some sort of satisfaction, who will sit in their living room and say 'Look I hate this son of a bitch as much as you do and I want to see him convicted too."' From a practical basis, having the detective hold your hand and introduce you helps get the family to open their home to you. I don't try to get people to sign official releases because that often makes them uncomfortable. Instead, I just use a letter printed on my letterhead. Besides, cops hate lawyers. They don't want to have anything to do with them and a formal, legal-looking release from an attorney would create problems.

"By the time I have the source and it's a 'go,' I've already gathered a lot of the material and have a good grip on the story. Next, I write a letter to the criminal—not their lawyer—because I want this guy to talk to me based on his decision alone. I am very careful when I write to him that I am not offering any promises, no cajoling, no seducing. Just a very short, clear letter that says I am writing a book about the murder of 'whomever' for which you have been convicted. If you want to say anything about this crime that reflects your point of view or any facts, I will represent it accurately in this book. That's it. I'm not giving anything up when I make that promise because readers don't care what the perpetrator feels. Then I have sources on the victim, the offender, and the investigation. Every crime is a triangle and you need those elements in there to make the triangle complete.

"When it comes to writing, I don't think about a plot until I'm well into it. By then I have read everything, have notebooks filled with material, have talked to everyone, and become one of the players. I just get so enmeshed in the story that writing it just seems to be the logical next step. I always have the contacts lined up and they know I'm going to be calling them back, so I choose where everything is going to go once I sit down to write. My viewpoint is established by then and I write dramatically and in scenes, so that seems most natural for me.

"One thing I always do is promise my detective and the victim's family that they can read every word I write before it goes to press. I'm the writer, so they can't control me or lead me, but since they were there and they lived it, they'll let me know if I'm not recreating it truthfully. This is important because it can be easy to get a wrong impression about an event that happened and then incorporate it into the text. I do this to make sure I recreate the story they tried to tell me as accurately as possible. This also gives me some of the creative license I need to re-create scenes because people don't care about exact words as much as they care about tone and intent of what is said. When I make that promise, those words seem to sweep away their last reservations about the fact that you, a stranger, won't go off and write something that is inaccurate and will ruin their lives. It may seem to be a small thing, but it has given me much better books than I would have had if I hadn't been willing to do it."

Brian Lane

A film school graduate turned lawyer, Lane began writing for Hollywood in 1980 after spending several years grinding cases through the Los Angeles criminal courts system. Unsure he could make it as a writer, he started out by doing adaptations of true stories at night while still practicing law during the day. Then he received a check for a single project that equaled his yearly salary and his legal career was effectively over. Since then, Lane has written or adapted material for crime-based television shows as diverse as *Colombo, Matlock,* and *Murder She Wrote,* among many others. In 1997, Lane drew national attention when he published *Cat and Mouse: Mind Games with a Serial Killer,* his account of the crimes of Bill Suff. He is currently at work on a book with serial killer Glenn Rogers about his cross-country murder spree.

* * * * *

"Although I had been writing crime-related pieces for years, *Cat and Mouse* came about because the Suff family wanted to sell their story. They went to *Hard Copy* and one of the producers there contacted his agent who got in touch with me. They had never talked to anyone prior to that, never said a word despite all of the media pressure during the trial. I talked to the brother and was fascinated with the story, but their motive was clear—they wanted to whitewash their own reputation after his conviction as a serial killer. The brother was very personable, but somewhat uninformed about all the details of the killings. Then I found out that Suff fancied himself as a writer and my interest deepened. I did a short proposal and pitched it in a Hollywood sort of way to Dove Books and they went for it. The only difficulty was getting into prison to spend time with Suff. There were also a lot of background files, endless transcripts, and I'm very meticulous. So I started to deal with Suff on a more personal basis, calling on the phone and visiting regularly to establish a relationship.

"The first thing I realized was that the game he was playing was all about manipulation. It's a mental chess game. He agreed over the phone that he would sign away the rights of attorney-client privilege so I could get access to the records, but when I started to get it off the ground I got a call where he was acting like a lawyer. He had talked to some copyright lawyer about intellectual property rights and had all the facts. I knew that I had to walk away from him and draw the line right there. I told him to forget about it and hung up. Two days passed and he was back on the phone begging me to do that. He was like a child who was totally egocentric. He got locked up in Riverside County jail (in Orange

County), but wasn't allowed out in the general population and he manipulated the system in his favor. It was a big deal for the jail to have a serial killer, and he exploited that. When I visited him I found him in a luxury suite complete with phone, television, lights, the works. He made friends with all the guards and had them on a string too. This is typical of guys like this, they're incredible manipulators.

"Right off the bat, I approached him on a writer-to-writer basis. I was very straight up and didn't pry. He was starstruck by that, by the fact that someone would consider him to be a writer, and he inadvertently began to reveal things. I offered my vulnerabilities right out front so he couldn't dig around for them and manipulate me. The question always became the same in each session: 'How far can I push him?' I always tried to maintain the sense that it could end any day, that I could never reveal that I needed his cooperation or that I needed or wanted to do the book. Internally, I had to keep telling myself that life would go on no matter what, that the project wasn't important to me, so that he couldn't manipulate me. Still, it got really creepy when I tried to get into his head. What he did to his victims wasn't fiction or an adaptation, it was real. The picking, the stalking, the killing, the posing, the redressing of the corpses, all of it was awful, but I was trying to find out what it all meant and I started trying to see the world his way, a way in which everything appears as a parallel universe. What I found was that he lives in a world that allows him to walk among us, but in which he sees something completely different and that he sees one world open up into the other continuously. He slips in and out of these realities and it is something that is hard to relate to. But I never felt threatened. One time we were alone in a small room off the library and we were looking out the window at a hill and he moved very close, unnaturally close, to me and I was nervous. When we were together I would often look at his hands and think 'Hey, those hands killed several dozen people—don't forget it.' But I also realized that he was on his best behavior because he was trying to prove that he was innocent.

"Researching the book took far longer than writing it, but the approach to telling a story is completely different than working on the type of series, movies, or docudramas that I usually do. That's because film is a collaborative medium more than it is a writer's medium. With a book, a writer works by himself and with an editor. In film, a writer has to hand over his work to directors and actors and producers, all of whom have to bend their efforts to the medium because the end product is pictures, not words. The writer winds up having his material being translated by a number of people because there is no such thing as a direct translation from one medium to another. A film is a different animal than a book, and it changes everything. I think that's one of the reasons that true crime writers are often so disappointed

211

when they see their work adapted, because they see it as it really was and the dynamics of film demands that it appear as something else.

"Part of that comes from the people who are actually doing the production, part is from the company that has funded it. Writers often wind up fighting with the production company or studio over the level of gore that goes in an adaptation. Naturally, they want to see everything in there for the impact it has, but the Standards and Practices department of a studio will weigh in and cut it out on the grounds of moral or image issues. These people are less concerned with what it takes to tell the story than who will be mad at them and give them bad press that could hurt the bottom line. Then there is the Errors and Omissions department that is concerned with accuracy and being sued after the fact. The primary way around these issues is usually to buy the rights either from the person who wrote the story or the survivor's family—or both—so you could dramatize it. The other approach would be to have two sources for everything you quote or anything that's potentially liable—just like a book. But that takes a lot more time. This used to be standard practice in docudramas where you had to use real names and real events when dealing with something like a star's love life or altercations with the law, but now it's more common to buy some rights from somebody. Take the Amy Fisher case as an example. You buy her side, buy Joey Buttafuco's side, buy the reporter's side of how they covered the story or wrote the book, and you're off the hook. Who's left to sue you? That's the way most companies operate these days and it is essential because any time you deal with real life it's not going to fit into a three-act structure. When adapting, you have to learn the geometry of what works—who did what to whom and why and when—then fit all of that within a standard three-act plot line. You have to get the dynamic down within that structure or it won't work. It's easy to capture the drama in a book because you can say it's real and you can use description and interior monologues to advance the story. But it doesn't work that way in an hour or two. So you compress characters and facts into one person or one scene to capture the essence of the story while remaining true to the main issue.

"As a television writer you're still looking at a three-act structure, but you have to put in false breaks to accommodate the commercials. That means you have to make the end of each section an important beat in the rhythm of the story and that's always been a big problem because most stories don't follow that pattern. The solution used to be that the first act was made really long because focus groups of audiences pointed out that you had to hook them by that point or you'd lose them. So a first act became twenty-five pages instead of fifteen, but that made you move all sorts of actions and motives up into it and then compress everything on the back end. It's the complete opposite of writing a book because the key event—a killing, a death, a loss of a child, a man finds out that his wife is a man, whatever—is all up front. That makes the second, third, fourth, and fifth acts a bastard to write because you've got to pad them to make up for all the material you've spent in the first. Then everything has got to be exactly to length because you're on television and they have to have those commercials at set intervals. The start is always the hardest part for me because you lose all the grounding and layering of the character's psychology and motivation that you can reveal slowly in a book. But that's what they use to sell the show and that's where you have to be by the end of act one or you'll lose the audience. It's a lot tougher than most people think and it's the main reason most book writers won't do adaptations of their own work."

Harry MacLean

A former lawyer and law professor who has served as a judge, Colorado's deputy attorney general, and general counsel for the Peace Corps in the Carter administration, MacLean came to writing as a second career in the early 1980s. Afraid that being a lawyer was all he was going to do with his life, he quit and began writing *In Broad Daylight*. The book landed on the *New York Times* bestseller list, won an Edgar Award, and was made into a television movie. Dedicated to accuracy, he is a dogged researcher known for his immersive style and isn't afraid to tackle controversial subjects. He followed the dramatic success of his first book with *Once Upon a Time: A True Story of Memory, Murder, and the Law* in 1994.

* * * * *

"I had been in the legal profession for fifteen years when I got back to Colorado after Carter left office. I wanted to write, so I started arbitrating just to make money because it was the least responsible job I figured I could hold. Then I read an article in a little box in *Time* magazine about a killing in Missouri and I was immediately interested in it. I thought, 'That is *my* story.' I have a master's degree in law and sociology and I had studied the impact of trauma on small towns and here was a bully who had been running around killing, raping, and marauding for twenty years. He was a hog farmer who was untouchable no matter how many witnesses saw him. Finally he met his end with a vigilante killing but the locals covered it up and it was the nature of that process that fascinated me. I moved to the town for two years and became part of the social fabric of the place. The town had only four hundred twenty people living in it and they were hostile to the press. At first, everyone thought I was undercover so it was tough. I had no prior experience as a writer and I did it stone cold. I worked on it six months before I thought I could do it. Then I got an agent through a friend of a friend, did a proposal, and sold it to HarperCollins. They didn't call it true crime then, they called it nonfiction but I was focused on the story and never thought of what I was doing as being part of any genre.

"I'm not sure if you could find a story like that today because the media sucks up the interest in crime cases like a sponge. Unfortunately, that wears out public interest in it and since a book takes two years, who wants to spend $29.95 on a book they think they know everything about after the fact? It's hard to sell that to the public, and it's harder to sell a classic, well-done, heavily researched true crime book these days as result. I regard the media as a curse for true crime writers because they screw up the facts, throw money around, sign people up to releases, misquote people, and really contaminate the scene. Another problem has been the rise of these instant books that bias the genre. Publishers already know that there will be two or three insta-books and they are reluctant to invest in a big hardback as a result. Plus it has changed the public's perception of true crime and they give us a bad reputation. All of this has gotten particularly bad in the last three or four years, so now I try to stay away from big cases. I routinely look through newspapers and magazines for stories, but my agent will call me with an idea he's heard or come across in something I haven't read. Sometimes an editor will get in touch about a possible project, but I've always found them to be lousy ideas. Just because it's an instantly graspable 'high concept' story that has good marketing potential doesn't mean it's going to be an interesting book at all. In many cases, it's just deep enough to be a magazine article. But any story, if it does something for you, if you've got the vision, the take on it, it's yours. Take a look at Mailer's *Executioner's Song* or Capote's book. I mean, who was Gary Gilmore? Or look at *In Cold Blood.* It was about a couple of losers. But Capote saw something in those characters and made them interesting. That's what makes the difference between a good and a bad book. In my mind the best true crime books are written by fiction writers, people who put themselves in the book with technique and a level of involvement that is foreign for a journalist who is trained to keep their distance. Journalists always write the worst true crime books because it's all research and facts and sensationalism and very little narrative technique. You need good people to make good characters and the technique to blow them up larger than life through your own psychology is what makes any story interesting.

"It's always people who make the story work, make it come alive, and you can't capture that over the phone or via e-mail. You've got to go out there, be there, and hang out in the bars, shoot pool, and get close to them. Drinking is often part of the job because it is where people relax and how they relax. It kind of bothers me because I'm fifty-four now and I can't drink as much any more. In Missouri, I'd drink fifteen beers and run into the bathroom and write down key words on a piece of paper to trigger my memory and then I'd go home and try to re-create it so I didn't forget. But you can't do my

217

immersive approach to research on nights and weekends. You don't know what you don't know, so how do you deal with that? My way is to just be there and see what happens. A lot of the big breaks I got happened just because of that. But you have to have a good intuitive sense about dealing with people. You have to figure out where they're coming from and be empathetic. So you talk about crops, coon dogs, their kids, whatever. A lot of time you only have thirty seconds to get across and connect with them, but you have to be there for those situations to occur. You cannot go in with a list of questions. You have to let things evolve. That's what kills journalists who try these books. You have to have a relationship and go back four, five, six times before someone will talk to you; it can't be fifteen questions and out the door. You have to let them go where they want in a conversation. I'll use a tape recorder or take notes, but at first I'll often have nothing and will tell people, say, that I'm interested the area and the lifestyle. I'll ask all sorts of general questions like 'What do you do on Sunday afternoon? What's the school like?'—really innocuous stuff, just to get a feel for the area. I'm always slow to pull that notebook out and when I do I'll often say 'Well, I have a bad memory, do you mind if I take a few notes?' People are lonely and love to talk, love to tell their story. I really don't say much. I just keep them going with things like 'Really? That right? How's that work?'

"I've always had great luck with cops, district attorneys, and defense lawyers. You have to convince them that you're not hooking up with one side or another. I drink all the time with cops because that's where you get the information. There's always a cop bar and I hang out in it. Sometimes the case would never come up, and then one day it will. I always take notes with cops because they're comfortable with that and they can deny it later. They hate tape recorders. But they're great characters and are often accessible after they see you around for a while. A lot of them see themselves as a character in a book, so if you say that you want to portray them as they are, they'll cooperate with you. A lot of time they do the heavy lifting and then the lawyers or the politicians will take credit. I typically hand out my book and they see that I'm legit. But if you don't have one, you have to make yourself as legit as you can at the time. Be honest; say you're totally committed. When I was doing my first book, people would ask 'Who's your publisher? What else have you done?' I'd always be straight up and positive with them about my ambitions and that was always enough.

"After you get all this information, one of the big challenges when it comes to writing is how do you make the people interesting? Sometimes there's a natural tension between good and evil in the personalities, but if it isn't there you have to create it. You have to make the reader care about one of the characters by making one of them sympathetic. Capote made people care about the bad guy. In my first book, I made the community itself the sympathetic character. A lot of stories will lack a good strong hero or a sympathetic character and if you can't figure out how to magnify someone's appealing traits, you will have a dumb story, a newspaper piece. That's the skill a writer brings to the story and it is something that has to be a conscious effort right from the beginning. You have to spin the trail out in a way that involves the reader, a way that characterizes a person's background that doesn't take away from the narrative. If you set your hook well enough up front, the reader will cut you a lot of slack. I've never made anything up like Capote did. After all, the family members that he quoted were dead. I always re-create with some direct knowledge of what took place at the time. But if it was a secondary or tertiary event, I would indicate it in some way. You have to be careful, and what people say in the foreword about how they did the research and where they took license is always interesting because it alerts the reader that you're making some stuff up, which is potentially hazardous to your credibility. If it's obvious, it doesn't matter. I'm very careful because I want every fact in there if someone ever challenges me. Whether it is an editor or another journalist, or a lawsuit, I want to be able to cite sources.

"My first book was made into a movie by New World with Brian Denahey starring in it. I had no experience with that world—the film and television industry—but everything bad I ever heard about it was true. I don't believe anything they say because it's all bullshit and the schmoozing and all the stereotypes are painfully accurate. When you've got something they're interested in, they're all on the come. Then you don't hear anything for six weeks and they can't remember your name. I was hired as a consultant on the project but they didn't pay much attention to me. I would review the script and do twenty pages of notes and they'd ignore it. Then I'd get the rewritten script back and the same thing would happen again. It was a lot of small detail, but they're not interested in that—things like they don't have dirt roads, they're all gravel in that part of the state; or whether or not a guy would wear a leather jacket. That's when I realized they didn't care, that they were writing something else and that was a more lasting reality. But they were nice to me on the set. You just have to stay out of the politics between the producers, directors, and stars. It was heavy. Once, the woman who was playing the lead came up to me and said, 'Don't you think that my character should have more to say?' Wanting to be nice, I said 'Sure,' so she went straight to the director and said 'The author said. . . . ' He was furious with me and told me to mind my own goddamn business. As soon as I backed out I had a great time chatting with people, and if I saw something that didn't make sense I'd keep my mouth shut. Plus they don't shoot sequentially, so it's hard to follow the process. It's a different world, one that revolves around money, and the egos are incredible. It's a brutal scene and it's not for everyone."

Darcy O'Brien

The son of two movie stars, O'Brien grew up in Holly-wood and was educated at Princeton. After college, he started out as an English professor writing criticism on English and Irish literature, but later turned to fiction. O'Brien wrote two novels and one, *A Way of Life Like Any Other,* won the 1978 Hemingway award. Encouraged, he wrote a third novel, which drew great reviews but had limited sales. Although he had settled in the Midwest, O'Brien had a college roommate who was making legal history in Los Angeles as the presiding judge in the notorious Hillside Strangler case. Fascinated with the drama of what was then the longest trial in the state's history, O'Brien returned to his hometown to write about it. *Two of a Kind: The Hillside Stranglers* became a national bestseller and was one of NBC's high-est-rated movies of the week. While a tenured professor at the University of Tulsa in Oklahoma, O'Brien has written a number of true crime books, including *Murder in Little Egypt, A Dark and Bloody Ground,* and the 1997 Edgar winner, *Power to Hurt.*

* * * * *

"At the start, I liked fiction because it seemed more noble than nonfiction. I came late to it in my mid-thirties, but I was encouraged with my early success. My novel *The Silver Spoon* sold out but wasn't reprinted and my third, *Margaret in Hollywood,* was praised but had lousy sales. Then the strangler case happened. I was fascinated because it was much more dramatic than any novel. I originally thought that I was going to write a novel on the stranglers, but then I realized that everyone would have thought that I was the psycho because I had created the characters. I thought that the novel just might be too unbelievable and, in fact, the truth was far wilder than fiction, so I decided to do a nonfiction account of the case. That's how I made the jump. "I did a proposal and got what I thought was a great advance, but I never thought that it would take five years to complete the book. At the time I never had heard the phrase 'true crime,' and when I did I thought that it was cheesy. I considered the book I was writing to be an exposé of evil because I was overwhelmed by the horror of these people. I wanted to show what the criminal mind can be like and to reveal disturbing things about the justice system. The book did very well and I started to get all sorts of tips on different cases and wound up doing another book on crime. My views evolved and by the time I was formally identified as 'a true crime writer' I had a very different view of the genre.

"While I didn't have any nonfiction experience when I started writing true crime, the two books that made me think I could write about the stranglers were Capote's *In Cold Blood* and Tommy Thompson's *Blood Money.* They showed me that you could use novelistic techniques and that it was possible to find enormous resonance to all areas of life in a criminal situation. I'm deeply interested in the interaction between different levels of society, and the court system is one of the few places you can see that these days. I'm attracted to the moral, legal, and social questions surrounding the cases I cover. It's never the crime *per se*, although there may be an interesting psychological angle to the events, but the issues that surround it, the things that make it possible socially and historically. I presented the strangler as symptomatic of a certain level of social and moral decay of Los Angeles. These people were not homeless or jobless or stupid. In fact, one was a successful businessman and one managed to fool a whole battery of psychologists and their sophisticated tests. It was really about the absurdity of the time we live in. No one can comprehend how people are capable of behavior like this. It's like Auschwitz in that regard, because no one can explain the sadism, the sexual component, the scientific element of seeing how long it took someone to die. By exploring the forces that created these crimes you could see how fragile civilization is and how one needs a moral code with which to live.

"Since the crimes don't matter to me, I always focus on the people and events around them. But there always has to be someone of intelligence in the story or I can't write it. I write novelistically and through people's minds, so if I can't relate to their minds, I can't do the book. The people are the key and I have to have an interest in both the villain and the hero, someone I can identify with in one way or another. In *A Dark and Bloody Ground*, I identified with the criminal, a woman who got involved with a bad crowd. She was this very complex, street-smart gal who got caught up in a bad scene and got swept away. She was smart and knew it, but she was not dead emotionally as a true criminal is— the psychopath, the sociopath—and I could sympathize with her problems. She was a fascinating character, as was the defense lawyer who got caught taking stolen money as his fee. This guy was a cross between Mark Twain and Shakespeare and it was absolutely riveting to see an 'honest crook' in action. He was just a great character. This pair just laid it all out for me, and didn't hold anything back. I got much more information than I would have asked for, all their motives, the works. But I'm also fascinated with the police. My grandfather was the police chief of San Diego and my dad always played the hero in movies, so I always liked cops, especially detectives. I got very close to Bob Grogin in the Strangler case and almost ruined my liver hanging out with him. My detectives are like Virgil leading Dante through the Inferno, they are the guides who take you through a dark underworld and come up with incredible insights into humanity. I think there's an old saying that claims 'The only people who truly understand human nature are homicide detectives and whores' and I think there's some truth in that. Still, it is amazing how emotional a detective can be while on a case. Every time Grogin found a body he thought of his daughter. But the pressure is enormous and a lot of these guys crack or give up and move away to the country.

"I usually start research by going to the area and finding people who really know about a place and there's always local historians around and they love to talk about it. They put you on to the right books and other people, so I never go to the library as a start. Once you know what you have to read you can get it via an interlibrary loan at your hometown and the local newspaper is a tremendous place to start. Never underestimate the resources of a local newspaper. I found a small local paper in Kentucky that won two Pulitzers. The people who run these papers are often very literate and literary because it's a labor of love and it is their life's work. But research takes time and I spend, on average, two years or more on a book. For *The Hillside Stranglers*, I took an apartment in Los Angeles and shared it. Expenses are business deductions, but the process is expensive and time-consuming. Whether it's fiction or nonfiction, I'm always interested in power—political and psychological—and the place. The setting is always a big part of my writing and you can see that in the books because I'm fascinated by all parts of America and the different local cultures it contains. I go deeply into the local history of a place, often spending a year researching it. The local language also fascinates me as a writer because I incorporate that in the dialogue used in the book. So researching these projects is expensive, but I would get bored writing about the same place or region all the time.

"When I interview people, I take notes rather than use a tape recorder for the same reason the FBI takes notes. A tape recorder tends to intimidate the subject or it encourages them to put on an act and become false. Also it can break and cause problems and I worry about that. I prefer to interview people in restaurants, bars, or in their houses because that's where they are most comfortable. It's also great to see their own houses because the symbolism of their own lives is in there and that's really valuable to a writer. That's something that a lot of nonfiction writers miss, the fact that everything's symbolic, even someone's ties, even what's *not* in their house. There's a story behind all of these things and it can help you discover more about their personalities and their lives.

"I'm conventional in terms of the way I write in that I believe things should have a beginning, a middle, and an end. With true crime, you've got to realize that you're not writing a journalistic news story. It's not just the action that you're trying to capture, it's the underlying motives and forces of what drives them. There is always a natural chronological order to these stories, but the way in which you reveal it to the reader shapes what you want it to mean. I always want the last chapter to tie together all the things that were in the book and what they mean on both a factual and thematic basis. But in

227

true crime, writing the endings is always tough. I mean, how do the people who are left deal with all of the tragedy that has happened in their lives? You may not even know where the ending is when you start the book—you may have a rough idea—but it can change as you write it. Publishers often ask for epilogues as an update and it's a legitimate request because readers have an interest in what happened to these people after the case was closed.

"All of my books have been optioned as films, but not all of them have been made. Although the NBC movie of the week based on *The Hillside Stranglers* got a twenty-three rating and was reshown a lot and that helped book sales. That was not a terribly unpleasant experience. But some of the adapted scripts are so horrible that you're glad they never made the thing. A lot of it has to do with who picks up the project. Some screenwriters can be asinine and have contempt for the material because it's 'just a job' and it shows in the writing. Others are deeply committed and want to do the best work possible. I had never been interested in doing my own adaptations, but I did try doing it once just to see what it was like. It was an agonizing experience and I realized right away that it was not my medium. It was like everything I had learned and struggled to achieve as a prose writer was worth nothing because the dialogue is completely different. There is an unreal sense of time with a narrative and film is real time. You have a simple equation: One minute equals half a page and you're bound by that. There were also network executives inter-fering and they were changing the motivation of the characters because they thought it was too dark even though it was based on real people. It was incredibly frustrating and I finally gave up trying to do it."

Jack Olsen

Widely lauded as one of the modern masters of true crime writing, Jack Olsen is a straight-talking journalist and former bureau chief for *Time* magazine. The author of more than thirty books, he has also written for *People, Vanity Fair, Paris Match, Reader's Digest, Life, Sports Illus-trated,* the *New York Times Book Review,* and many other publications. His best-known books include *Son: A Psy-chopath and His Victims, Predator, "Doc": The Rape of the Town of Lovell, The Bridge at Chappaquiddick,* and *Silence in Monte Sole.* Olsen's works have been widely adapted as television movies; he has been nominated for five Pulitzer Prizes and is the winner of several Edgar and American Mystery awards for true crime writing.

* * * * *

"In many ways, I've been interested in true crime writing all my life. My fascination with it started while I was a student at the University of Pennsylvania. I went on a field trip to the Holmsberg Penitentiary as part of a criminology course I was taking and discovered that it was filled with a bunch of guys just like me. Before I went inside I thought I was going to see a bunch of stubble-bearded, snaggle-toothed, ugly guys—criminals—but they all looked like me and my family and my friends. They looked like regular suburban people and I became fascinated with the question of why they were inside and I was outside. Although I've written just about everything, crime permeated my career as a journalist. I wrote a column called 'Cops and Crime' for the *San Diego Journal*, I covered crime for the *Chicago Sun Times*, and I started writing true crime exclusively in 1982. I try to make a living writing true crime, but I'm also trying to leave something behind me as a legacy. My emphasis is on what made the criminal a criminal. I'm the guy who started the trend where the story explained where the criminal came from, what the family dynamic was, and what the background issues were to give the reader an idea of how they became that way. At first, publishers complained that my approach stopped the action and action was what they thought true crime was supposed to deliver. So I had quite a fight on my hands when I first started to do it, but now if you don't explain all that you get criticized for it. It's what people have come to expect from the genre, an explanation of the criminal mind, of criminal behavior, and how to avoid people like that. That's an advance in the field that I'm proud of.

"These days there's a huge schism in true crime writing. It used to be that there was the old kind of true crime that was grossly embellished. Then along came *In Cold Blood*. It was a great book, even a work of genius, but the ending is completely fabricated. That sort of started this wave, because before that there was just the *Boston Strangler* and similar titles that were hard-driving journalism. But Capote's success issued a license to blend fact and fiction and present it as truth. It reached its nadir last year with Lorenzo Carcaterra's *Sleepers*, but the only good thing about that book was that it started a trend back to solid journalism. That's all I've ever done and can do. I've been an Edgar judge and I read fifty or sixty books a year and I see a very vigorous trend back towards good reporting. But it isn't selling as well because people have gotten used to being entertained by things that aren't entirely true. Since I'm seventy-two, it's not a problem that's going to be solved in my lifetime, but the trend towards solidly researched work is clearly taking hold. Just look at the 1997 Edgar winner, *Power to Hurt* by Darcy O'Brien, or last year's winner, *Circumstantial Evidence* by Pete Earley. One of the best books I've read was *All God's Children* by former *New York Times* reporter Fox Butterfield. There's been a real resurgence of quality and the level of writing is very high, but there's still a lot of lousy material coming on the low end of the market under the guise of true crime.

"I never spend less than two years on a book, sometimes more, so it's hard to make it financially and I think it's getting harder to make it as a true crime writer. People have to walk a fine line about what they're going

231

to write—something for the ages or something to pay the rent. I try and compromise between the two by focusing on the human relations that surround a crime. That's where your book is. It's not just the crime, it's all in the background dynamics that created it. But you've still got to tell a story. That's the first thing I tell anyone, that there's got to be a reason for the reader to turn the page. That's rule numbers one through eleven, because if you don't do it, nothing will happen and no one will buy the book. These days, television has indoctrinated audiences and that has changed what people will put up with. Now you've got to give them a hook to get them into the story. Another one of my rules is that you've got to show the subject in action to get the reader involved in both the character and the story. You've got to hook them until they are so interested that you can give them ten pages of background and they won't mind it. It might take forty pages to get them to that point where they are asking 'where'd this guy come from?'—but then you're ready to get to the interesting part. You've got to show your characters doing interesting things and make sure that they're interesting people before you can get into the expository biography and off the main narrative. You've got to show the guy in action so the reader *wants* the description. But if someone wants to write true crime, they have to learn to differentiate between something that will last a hundred years and something that is fast-paced and will make the money now. They will have to confront that problem every single day and there's no room for idealism. No matter how much you want to teach the public about crime and criminals, you've got to get them to want to read the book.

"Research is the key to a good true crime book. A lot of it is preliminary research because there are a lot of very sensational crimes that involve unsensational people, people the reader doesn't want to read about. You have to be very careful about judging that before you commit to a book. In my mind, the trial transcript is the least important thing of all because the stuff that's really interesting to me usually isn't admissible. It's always the background material that gives you the story. On the whole, I'm bored by transcripts, but they are good for sources and you can't be sued for anything in them and that's important, so they do play a role.

"I get cooperation from sources by hanging around. That's the school of interviewing I came from. I'm a hanger. I don't quiz people, I sit down and have a conversation. You've got to develop a spark of empathy or you're dead. Sometimes I go back four or five times before I get something good. When I was working on 'Doc' I was dealing with a Mormon woman who I knew was the key to the story. I talked to her five times and didn't get anything, just childhood stuff, bunny tales, memories, the kind of useless crap that just fills the air. One day she needed to drive seventy miles to Billings for bread and didn't have a way to get there. I offered her a ride and I hooked up a mike on her collar. I told her that if she said anything important, I'd have it; if not, no big deal. Ten miles out of town she starts to tell me about a man in town who abused her, her siblings, and others in the town and had never been arrested or even charged. That was the key to a lot of the story because it revealed the background against which this doctor had been raping people while doing gynecological exams on them. You can't just sit down and give someone the third degree to get them to tell you that. But it unlocked everything else in the story.

"Criminals are tougher 'cause they're psychos and they want to control everything. In face-to-face interviews, you've got to act like you like them. You've got to be somewhat hypocritical and be friendly no matter how repellent they are. What saves me is that I don't differentiate between people. We all start as seven, eight, or nine pounds of protoplasm and then all sorts of forces are brought to bear: Social, genetic, educational, familial, sexual, and so on. That's what shapes people and their actions. I'm a determinist and I know that these people are the result of the forces that are inflicted upon them. I don't sit down with utter contempt for them. I mean, I hope that they're behind bars and I don't want them out, but I never think 'you rotten son of a bitch' when I sit down to interview them. I get in contact with the criminal however I can, through the attorney, the wife, the penitentiary officials, whoever has access. But you're dealing with psychopaths who like to run you and you have to be aware of it. You've got to have a great bullshit detector in this business and see through it, or you can get into trouble fast.

"I don't mind changing names of characters because a lot of people won't cooperate unless you do that. When I wrote *Son*, I started sticking an asterisk next to a changed name the first time it was used, and a lot of people will do this or italicize the name the first time it appears. What you want to do as a writer is to hold the explanations to a minimum while remaining truthful. The reader doesn't care about things like a changed name, especially if you let them know. If you change the timeline or take liberty with a quote, you have to let the reader know that too. I believe that as long as you're honest on that level you can have a lot of latitude in how you shape a story. I also think that every true crime author needs a few sentences to give the reader a few clues to his method in an acknowledgments section. Another thing that is important is an epilogue. I started the prologue-epilogue trend in true crime and I think that the epilogue is important because there is always a lapse between finishing the book and its publication. It brings the reader up to date on all the characters and where they are now, things like 'This guy's in prison serving a life sentence, this gal got remarried, this detective retired,' and so forth. Readers like that and it's a very effective technique in terms of closure for both the book and the story."

Fred Rosen

With a Master's in Fine Arts in film from the University of Southern California, Rosen originally wanted to be in television. But his return to New York City led to a career in journalism as the photography columnist for the *New York Times* and a teaching position at Hofstra University. He also wrote for all the national photo magazines, but hated the work because it lacked creativity. In between assignments and classes, Rosen wrote a novel that he tried to sell to Pinnacle. During that process he met editor Paul Dinas, who told him about a book concept about doctors and patient abuse. It led to a successful anthology that led to other projects such as the true crime paperback classic *Lobster Boy,* a murder story set in a world of carnival freaks and sideshow workers. The book was unusual because in the course of researching it, Rosen uncovered evidence that convicted the killer. His other books include *Gang Mom, Chameleon,* and *The Pennsylvania Skinhead Murders,* among others; his original screenplay *A Woman Like Me* is being developed by Smith-Hemion Productions, and ABC is developing *Chameleon* into a movie of the week.

* * * * *

"I learned how to write true crime from reading Ross MacDonald and Raymond Chandler and I always wanted to write something that provided that same sense of compelling mystery. But the thing that really affected my writing was Tom Wolfe's essay on the 'New Journalism.' It was on how to write nonfiction with a narrative technique and it changed everything for me. Unfortunately, most publishers want you to be down and dirty when you're doing a true crime book, particularly when it is a paperback. They want to focus on the details of the crime because that's what they feel the reader wants. I've found that as long as you deliver that you can pretty much do what you want with the rest of the story. That doesn't mean you can quote the *Great Gatsby*, but I've become aware of what I can do in terms of style and structure. One of the problems with the current market for true crime is that it is glutted with sensational stories that are very shallow and poorly written. There's no behind-the-scenes examination of the characters' motivation that makes the story compelling and interesting. Then there's the growing number of instant 'cut-and-clip jobs' or books that are half fiction to satisfy the public's desires for sensationalism. That kind of stuff is really clogging up the market and it drives down the money a writer can get and gives the genre a bad name.

"When looking for material, I use all sorts of sources. The place where you find stuff is by looking at newspaper databases and I use the Internet to look at stories. Every day, I'll go through a couple of papers and if something interest me I'll download it and look at it later. These days, I look for something that will be a good read and stories that I think I can get behind and get to the motivation that the reporter didn't have time to bring out. I want to create a setting that gives some order to the universe, some sense of explanation about how these horrible things came to pass. It takes time, but after a while you develop an 'eye' for what works and what doesn't. The first thing I'd tell someone is 'go to AP wire and look around.' I found the *Lobster Boy* story in a newspaper while on vacation in Florida. I called my editor and he loved the idea, but I had no idea what I was getting into. I knew it had this freaky background with the carnival people, but I never really thought about the social environment and their personal deformities. I was just looking at the crime and that aspect was window dressing. What I care about is the 'why' of the case because the reader wants to know 'why did this happen?' I'm good at talking to people who usually don't talk to reporters and then explaining it in a way that makes sense. The key to the case revolved around a videotape that was played in court without sound. It was the Lobster Boy wrestling with his son in what appeared to be a violent manner. But the tape I received had sound and it completely changed the meaning of the tape. All the press people got a copy, but this was the only one that had a soundtrack. I approached the prosecutor and told him about it. I knew that the defense knew that it had sound and that they had copied it without sound and when they played it in court they turned the sound down. All of a sudden I was in the murder trial and I had the pivotal piece of evidence. That was a lot more than I had bargained for.

"I had a clear-cut idea of what right and wrong was, but I didn't know what to do. Would they come after me? Was I in danger? Then I realized that I did not stand above the law, that there was always a right or wrong and I had an obligation here. So I went to the defense attorney and asked him if there was sound on the tape and, if so, what did it say? I did it to give him one last chance. He declined to answer the question and that was that. I turned it over to the prosecutor and when it was introduced in court, I was cited as the source. While the jury was being ushered in, the defense attorney came over and demanded to know where I got it. I said 'From you,' and he said 'You had the audacity to turn it over to the prosecution?' I said, 'Well, you had the audacity to turn down the sound.' I thought he was going to hit me, but the tape turned the tide and the killer was convicted. It was something I never expected and I have to say that becoming involved in a case is certainly one of the downsides of writing true crime. It's exciting because you really immerse yourself in another world, but it takes a toll on your personal life. It impacts your family because you're always dealing with lowlifes and killers and there is a heavy emotional aspect and that can leak into your personal life.

"One of the things I really love about these books is the research. I love the field work more than anything because writing is a very solitary process and it gets you out to talk to people. I sometimes cover the case while it's going on and I think it makes a difference. In many cases, it helps in terms of getting a better grip on the story because you've got everyone in one place at the same time. You've got the dynamic of the trial and people's personalities come out under that stress. It's quite revealing, plus you get to see the wheels of justice turning. But it's tougher to do from a cost basis for the writer because it takes more time and costs more money and you've got to look at the advance you've negotiated and how far that will go. But I always do a lot of legwork when it comes to getting sources.

"When I go to interview the police I always dress in a suit and tie because it's a sign of respect for the uniform. I try to relate to what they do and I always ask them how the work affects their personal lives. Detectives are usually college educated, often with a master's degree, and I try to relate on an intellectual level. I also use humor a lot because it's important to get them laughing. They all have this remarkable ability to detach from what they do, and humor plays a big part in that. I tell them that I don't have a predisposition, I'm just here to find out what's going on and that I'm not interested in what the local media is putting out. I learned from Joe McGinniss's problems with *Fatal Vision* not to promise anything to anyone—ever. I try to be empathetic whenever I can because you can't judge people. That's the worst thing you can do, especially with the criminals. It's hard to interview the criminal while they're on trial, but it's always hard when interviewing a criminal because they're ultimately psychopaths that don't really make sense in the way we understand it. They don't have feelings and they have no guilt. I believe that they are born with that and the conditions of their lives contribute to it. I mean, we all know people who are a little nuts and who do things that we don't understand, but they don't go out and kill someone in cold blood.

"I've been pretty successful in having my projects optioned for adaptations. I'll negotiate an option on a book for a year, with a year renewal. I have set fees: X amount for a miniseries, another for a movie of the week, and another for a feature film. I also try to attach myself as a creative consultant so I'll have some input on the outcome of the product and I get a fee for that. It's important to understand that it's all Monopoly money in the movie business. Hollywood people always throw big figures around, but who cares? The fact is 90 percent of the things that are optioned don't get made. So it's just a game, but the game ends when it gets a green light and goes into production. Writers can get taken in by all those zeroes in a figure really easy, but I've found that you can't take it too seriously. But you do have to be serious when dealing with producers. You have to play it straight with them because their desire to get a movie made is perhaps more insatiable than anything in the publishing business. Since it is far more difficult to get something made in the film business and they're trying to get that done, they take themselves very seriously. The irony is that they dress less formally, but they are far more formal when it comes to doing business. They don't make as many jokes and I would never talk to them in the same way I talk to an editor. I've found that publishing is much more democratic. Still, I like to work in both mediums. Each offers its own challenges and although the writing will be remembered longer than the show, the show is more fun to make and is more lucrative."

Ann Rule

A former Seattle policewoman who has become one of the nation's foremost true crime writers, Rule has written ten national bestsellers and countless articles. Her first book, *The Stranger Beside Me,* dealt with the horror of realizing that her friend and co-worker, Ted Bundy, was a depraved serial killer. Rule's other books include *A Rose for Her Grave, You Belong to Me, If You Really Loved Me, Everything She Ever Wanted, Small Sacrifices, Dead by Sunset,* and *Possession.* Considered to be a leading expert on serial killers, she gives regular seminars to law enforcement professionals around the nation on the individuals she's studied as well as on topics such as sadistic sociopathy and women who kill.

* * * * *

"My interest in true crime is probably genetic. My grandfather was a sheriff, my uncle was a sheriff, another uncle was a coroner and I spent every summer growing up in the 1940s visiting them. Because it was a mom-pop operation where the jail, office, and house were all under one roof, I got to see everything. My grandmother cooked for the prisoners, I passed the food through the slot, and I listened to prisoners as they were interviewed. When I used to pass out the food to the criminals they were always very nice and very polite. Sometimes they would give me nickels for ice cream. I thought they looked just like my dad or my uncles and I couldn't figure out what made them different. A murderess taught me how to crochet and she was the nicest person. She had caught her husband with another woman and she called it 'justifiable homicide.' She'd never done anything else wrong in her life. I was fascinated about why people could grow up to be criminals, intrigued by what made them that way. I was also amazed at how my grandfather employed forensic science in his investigations.

"I got a college degree from the University of Washington in creative writing, but the minute I graduated I signed up with the Seattle Police Department. There were eighteen women at the time and we worked on sex cases and juvenile crimes, more of what would be called social work today. I was on the force for only eighteen months because I couldn't pass the civil service exams.

I'm myopic in the extreme and I couldn't get past the eye test. It was a big disappointment for me and I was so heartbroken that I couldn't even drive by the police station for five years. After I left the force, I started out writing true confession stories for magazines such as *Modern Romances, My True Stories*, those sorts of publications. I was raising four children and I wrote what I thought would sell. But in 1969 I started writing for the *Detective Magazine* chain. *True Detective* had been in business for seventy-five years at that point and the *New York Daily News* frequently syndicated their stories. I started out doing one five-thousand-word article a week and then started using pseudonyms and writing between two and three stories a week to make more money. I wrote fourteen hundred of those five-thousand-word articles and got to know people in every police department from the Canadian border to southern Oregon and Montana. It was funny, but when I went back to the Seattle police as a writer I was welcomed into the homicide unit, a place where I was never allowed while on the force.

"Judging by the mail I get and the response to my books, I think the genre is as solid as ever and will never die. Readers send me news clippings and letters about potential cases all the time. When I'm looking for a story I read papers, a lot comes through the Internet, and cops call all the time with cases. I go through over three hundred cases before I pick one to work on. I'm not looking for the high-profile case—I turned down several

offers to do a book on the O.J. Simpson case—I'm looking for a case with a certain type of character. I like the
protagonist, either male or female, to have a certain set
of qualities. Things like physical attractiveness, education, money, charisma, charm, success, all the things that
people want in their own lives. It always makes the
reader wonder 'Hey, they had it all, how could they do
that? How could they throw it all away?' The simple fact
is that we are more interested in someone like a Donald
Trump committing a horrible crime than a bum. The
beautiful people make the best subjects for true crime
and I like women protagonists because when they're bad,
they're *really* bad! I'm also looking for cases that are so
convoluted that the story will a carry itself because just
when you think it's run out, they do something else.
That's why I love true crime, because if it was a novel it
would be too contrived. But the fact that it's real makes
it much more compelling. When I find the right case,
the hairs stand up on the back of my neck. So I look for
a lower-key story that is utterly fascinating so that when
the reader starts reading they won't know from page one
who did it. I like to string it out over the whole book.
Most of the people I've written about folks haven't heard
of. When I wrote *Small Sacrifices* it took me three years
because the killer talked so much. The publisher didn't
like it because she wasn't well known and the crime
wasn't well known, but it sold more than any other book.
I think it was because women are the majority of true
crime readers. The gentlest of people are fascinated with

true crime and my readers don't kill things, yet they are fascinated with the 'why' behind someone committing crime.

"When true crime became really hot in the late 1980s, everybody jumped on the bandwagon and the level and quality of the writing really went down. People always told the crime in the first chapter and it was all downhill from there. A lot of writers thought that all you had to do was repeat a police report and then add a lot of gore. I don't write about the 'how' of it—I always focus on the 'why.' Instead, I always put something on the first page that is so tantalizing that the reader knows that something horrific has happened, but they don't know what. Then I will go back through the lives of the people involved and weave them together until it culminates in the crime. Then I shift to a more linear narrative through the investigation and the trial. I always include the trial because it's an essential part of the book.

"If I did research for a straight stretch it would be at least six months on average for a book. I get everything, all the newspapers, the follow-ups from the cops, input from other reporters on the case who can offer insights that you might not have—everything. I use maps a lot and I have a program in my computer that will give me the topographic nature of the area and the street layout. I also use weather reports and one of my favorite things is to go back to the crime scene and use a timeline book that will help recreate the era. I always go to the place where things will happen so the reader can see it through my eyes. It all adds up. But I try to have three sources for everything. Recently, I got videotapes of the police interrogation from the prosecutors and it made a huge difference, but I still went on to interview the criminal, her husband, and his mistress to confirm certain things.

"When covering a trial, I usually buy the transcripts. But I often go to court with an assistant who will also take notes on the testimony, people's clothes and expressions, little things that I might miss. It may sound funny, but I'm always scared and bashful every time I approach a prosecutor in court. I tell them that I don't want to make them nervous, but I have to do my job and 'I promise I won't talk to any of your witnesses until after the case has been resolved.' With the victim's family, well, they see me in court every day and know that I care enough to be there. We talk in the halls, but often never about the case. Instead it's just chatting about the weather, sports, and so on, and by the end of the trial, we're friends. With the cops and prosecutors, I wait till the case is over so they can relax because everything's on the public record and they can talk about it. Every time I start a book, I'm always terrified that I'll never find out enough because it's often about secrets that people have hidden for years. But I stay with it and it's amazing what will turn up if you stay there long enough. When people know that you really care, they will tell you anything. If someone says 'Don't use this,' I won't. But everyone has a story to tell and they love to have an audience. I usually use a tape recorder and I'm always amazed at how many people will let you do that. On a recent case in Kansas city I couldn't go in as a media visitor because they don't want to make the prisoners famous. As a regular visitor you can't bring in any writing materials, so I went out to the car and taped it. I prefer to use tape because I like to have absolutely accurate quotes, but I don't transcribe them. I just listen to them, especially during long car rides. I listen to them over and over so they become part of my consciousness.

"All the criminals have talked to me except one, but her daughter talked to me and turned over some tapes that revealed her inner nature. If you stay with a case long enough, something always turns up. I usually contact the criminal by sending a letter to the prison. They usually like to talk, but you always hear the same script over and over: 'I'm innocent. The D.A. made a mistake and doesn't want to admit it. The cops are crooked. You ask my family, they'll tell you what a nice guy I am,' that sort of thing. These guys are often very smooth and engaging and I have to remain focused on the physical evidence, which is often directly at odds with what they are saying. I watch their eyes because the eyes of a true sociopath don't allow you to see anything beyond the facade. It can be easy to get taken in by some of them unless you remain alert.

"Beyond my books, I am under contract with Colombia Tristar as an executive producer on all my own material. *Small Sacrifices* was a miniseries in 1989, *Dead by Sunset* came out in 1995, and I currently have two projects in pre-production at NBC right now. But I don't do the adaptations. I don't have the time and a screenwriter has a completely different approach. That kind of writing is different, there's no description, it's all dialogue, and they have to leave out a lot of the background stuff to fit into the format.

"I can accept that certain things are fictionalized, but I once got to page sixty-three of the screenplay adaptation of one of my books before I got to anything that I had written or was even true. Hollywood is not a happy place for book writers because everyone wants to put their own spin on it. I moved down there for eight months once to work on a project and that was enough. I have really good agents, I have the protection of my deal, and I'm treated very well now, but I love the book world a lot more."

Chapter Nine

FROM PROPOSAL TO PUBLICATION

True Crime Editors Tell What It Takes

A s any writer will tell you, having a good editor is as important as being able to find and tell a good story. Whether it starts with a pitch from an agent or a proposal that comes directly from a writer, every publishing contract starts with getting an editor interested in your idea. In each case, the editor must then sell the concept to an internal editorial committee as well as to the publisher's sales and marketing departments. Once a proposal is accepted, an editor then helps to shape and refine your work into a book that people will pay to read. While the nuances of this role vary widely between individual editors and writers, the goal is always the same—to make the manuscript as strong and compelling as possible.

Beyond issues such as structure and syntax, no book can succeed in the marketplace without strong support from a publisher's publicity and promotions departments. Most editors play an often-overlooked role in these areas by coordinating a project with the efforts of the promotional team and writing catalog copy that will help the sales force. In the increasingly competitive environment of book publishing, many have expanded their roles in these areas and won't take on a project unless they can gauge the marketability of a writer's idea right from the start.

While publishing is a cyclical business—one where trends come and go and come back again—true crime has proved to be a source of steady sales figures. Still, many publishers continue to embrace a "bestseller" mentality that limits their willingness to take on books about smaller cases or from unknown writers, and the nature of the genre is one that many editors are not comfortable with. But there are a handful of men and women who have come to specialize in editing true crime, and their insights regarding both the subject matter and the techniques for effectively bringing it to life can help every writer. They know what works and they know what they're looking for. Just listen.

Paul Dinas

Editor-in-Chief, Kensington Books, New York

As a man who is quick to claim, "I've been interested in the violent and the perverse all my life," Dinas has a natural affinity for the genre. Originally hired to work on fiction projects, his enthusiasm for grisly topics led to his first true crime assignment. As the market for these books rapidly expanded in the late 1980s and early 1990s, the field quickly became his specialty and he has produced a steady string of successful titles. Dinas has edited works in both hardcover and paperback, including recent works such as Lowell Cauffiel's *Masquerade*, Joel Norris's *Jeffery Dahlmer*, Phil Carlow's *The Night Stalker*, Fred Rosen's *Lobster Boy*, Aphrodite Jones's *Cruel Sacrifice*, and Tom Jackman's *Right to Burial*.

* * * * *

"I define true crime as 'sensational nonfiction.' It is nonfiction that has some criminal activity attached to the story and it has been a loosely recognized genre since the tabloids began in the 1920s. Lurid true stories always generated interest and have existed in a variety of formats over the years, including everything from true detectives, pulp books, and magazines to more literary works. What makes it different now is that it became a bona fide genre in books in the publishing industry's eyes from *Helter*

253

Skelter on. Before that it was a catch-all category that ranged from murder to kidnapping, but it really shifted and consolidated into an accepted genre with the success of the Charles Manson and Ted Bundy books.

"True crime has always been popular because there is a very dark need in this country to peek behind the veil of normality and look at the dark side of life. People are in need of the extra thrill. Drugs don't do it, adultery doesn't do it, sex doesn't do it any more, and, as strange as it sounds, violence has become a form of personal exploration. There is something about it that lets people experience that need for a lurid thrill that you can't get any more with things that used to be taboo. True crime attracts people because it is attendant to that need. It gives a fix on a lifestyle that most folks don't have access to. Readers keep asking themselves 'how can they do that?' while exploring all sorts of dark feelings and behaviors without having to cross that line themselves. Plus there is a need for control. People want to see the hounds of justice prevail; to experience the feeling that when something goes wrong, or something truly horrible happens, that someone will be caught and punished; that the world, the system, works the way it is supposed to and will protect them from these evil forces.

"From a story standpoint, I believe that the current core market for true crime wants the most vicious and bizarre cases possible. Quite frankly, if *In Cold Blood* came across my desk tomorrow I don't know if I would publish it. It's not intense enough, bloody enough, or

254

lurid enough to meet the public's demand. People are looking for something over the top and, particularly in the paperback market, the literary approach has been passed by the public's demand for blood. As a rule, I turn down books that only have one victim or projects that have a mundane means of murder like guns or strangling. I'm looking for the upper range of perversity in a crime, or a sense of obscurity that makes it unique. In my experience, all of the good stuff happens off the beaten track—from along the lonely byways of northern Florida or in the hinterlands of Minnesota. I look for a uniqueness in the setting and then some extreme violence or a new angle to the story. But you have to be careful when picking a case because some larger crimes are often so overexposed, so sliced and diced by the media, that it is hard to get a completely unique perspective. But if you look hard enough, it's usually there. For example, I got the husband in the Susan Smith case to do a project which provided a whole different angle on the case. That was different enough to merit a book because it hadn't been heard before and that's what I look for when reviewing new projects.

"When I consider a book, I like a full proposal with a narrative synopsis of seven to ten pages with the whole story, plus some visuals. I weigh the impact of a story and look at the depth of it. A guy shooting his wife because he has a girlfriend on the side is nothing because you need a lot of levels to the crime, it can't be two-dimensional. I also need to have a conviction because these stories don't really work without one. But people are jumping in earlier and earlier due to media coverage. Now when a guy is arrested for a crime there is a book proposal right away, which is good for me, but tough for the writer. We have a conviction clause that states if the guy is not convicted of the crime, then we have the choice to cancel the book. This is for legal reasons because you can't have someone killing someone only to get away. Closure is very important in true crime because people don't want to be left hanging, they want to know the system works.

"I'm happy to deal with people direct, but I often buy from agents because they know what sells and they get a writer a better deal. Once we reach an agreement, I talk to the writer and make sure that they understand what we need in the book and that they get all the transcripts and the photos attached to the case. I think this is important because some writers leave the pictures to last. They are often incredibly hard to get because they are the key to exposure. Everybody has a big moral agenda about exploiting the crime these days and that makes it tough to get crime scene shots or autopsy shots. In many cases, the families either want a lot of cash or they are really reticent about making the picture public. We used to be able to get photos from the local papers for free, but now many of them view these as profit centers that they can milk for cash or they simply won't release them. Since you need a shot of the perpetrator and hopefully some of the crime scene to go into the book, this poses a problem for the publisher. In my opinion, the writer should be worried about getting the pictures before he or she worries about anything else. When buying true crime, people often look at the pictures first and if they don't grab them, they put it down. Writers need to know that—pictures are at least 60 percent of the initial draw of the book in the store and you can't sell a paperback if you don't have solid pictures. This may seem trivial, but it is a key issue because what makes a book different is that it delivers the things you can't get anywhere else. This includes things like the autopsy pictures, the severed breasts of prostitutes, the slashed throats—things you'll never see on TV or in the newspaper or anywhere else.

"I work with established authors but also deal with new writers all the time. True crime is a genre that is best suited for journalists, but one that is tougher for novelists because they don't research as thoroughly—even though they think they do. True crime writers need to put a lot of work into a project. The chronology and details of a story are important and many writers can be lousy about consistency of names, facts, and dates. This can be misspelling or simply not cross-checking things. Names are the worst and have to be triple-checked because you can't make an assumption that just because a name is in a trial transcript that it's spelled correctly or that a date is right. Trial transcripts are not proofread to make sure that dates are right or names are correctly spelled, so you can't rely on them. You have to go the extra mile and check it yourself. But I've found that a lot of first-time writers are so eager to be published that they are willing to put that extra effort into a project. Quite often it is a local access to people that they bring to the story, but they then find that they don't know how to structure it and aren't ready for the length of time involved. True crime writing is hard work and takes a lot more time and effort than most people think. My advice to writers is always the same: Pick your crime wisely before you put together a proposal. Look at it from a reader's standpoint. Is it complex and multilevel enough to merit a book? Do your homework and be ready for all the questions that I'm going to ask about motive and dates and facts and the background of the characters. Then try to line up the visuals as early as possible. Get access to the cops involved in the case, sign the family to releases. You can make all the promises in the world, but I'm looking for the thoroughness that is the cornerstone of professionalism. I want a writer who has the ability to select the relevant facts from a lot of information and is able to tell the story in a clear and dramatic way. People are going to read this book for information it contains as well as the story. They want to see how it impacted people's lives because that is what they can relate to and I need to see that from a writer before I'll take on a book with them.

"The high-water mark for true crime was 1993, when you could publish anything and have a success. This was when the Jeffery Dahlmer and John Wayne Gacy cases were in the news and true crime was white hot. You couldn't sell enough of it. I think that it has peaked since then from overexposure and media saturation. When it got hot, the TV magazine shows created their own subgenre to capitalize on the public's interest in true crime and reality-based events and this shift has been both the biggest booster and biggest enemy of true crime books. On one hand, the attention can drive sales through media coverage; on the other, these shows sweep into town and sign up all the rights and the principals involved in the case for their broadcasts. This effectively leaves the writer out in the cold and the public is left feeling that they know all they want to know about a case before a book can come out. This level of competition is really tough for publishers because they can't compete on a financial level or in terms of a timely delivery of information and it has really impacted the market for true crime books. One of the responses to that has been an increase in 'insta-books.' Unfortunately, these are often cut-and-paste projects that come out while the case is ongoing, but I look for closure. The insta-book trend has dropped off because people realize that it's just a rehash of what's for free in the daily news or *Time* magazine and they buy a book to deliver some new information. If it doesn't have that, it won't sell. This has created an environment where true crime is a tougher sell because, while the consuming public wants it, the publishing industry thinks it's passé as a result of the immediacy of the media overexposure. But the fact is a consumer *will* buy the book because television can only show so much and the book has more information. Yet book buyers in the stores think that it won't sell because everyone has seen it or heard it all before and they only order a few copies. This effectively lowers the numbers on the shelf which, in turn, drives the overall trend of sales down. Then these lower numbers reinforce the belief that the market has dropped off and the consumer interest isn't there anymore. In many ways it is a self-fulfilling prophecy. But you can get things out of a book that you can never get from the paper or from television and it will always have the grisly edge that true crime readers love."

Doug Grad

Senior Editor, Ballantine Books, New York

Grad started editing true crime by default. He inherited a book on serial killer Ted Bundy from another editor and found the project challenging. It was followed by a proposal from an undercover narcotics agent that he liked and the two wound up producing several books together. Grad found that he was fascinated by the contrast between the seemingly ordinary subjects and the horrible crimes they committed and the fact that true crime books often contained classic themes that revealed a greater truth about humanity. He began to do more work in the area, editing Vincent Bugliosi's *And the Sea*

Will Tell, the reprint of Nick Pron's *Lethal Marriage,* Rodney Barker's *Dancing with the Devil* and *Broken Circle,* Robert Cullen's *Citizen X,* and David Simon's *Homicide,* among many others.

* * * * *

"I think the first thing that sets true crime apart as a genre is the presence of a truly horrific crime—something completely out of the ordinary. Horrific crimes have always been there, and there have been a number of 'crimes of the century,' but the media spotlight on this behavior has intensified and increased the public's attraction to it. I'm not sure why, but in America there's a fascination with the dark side of human nature and that's reflected in the media. The O.J. Simpson trial was an example of the media's fascination with this and it's helped to make the genre popular with a new generation of readers. In the 1950s we had a lot of classic lurid crime fiction, but now the emphasis is on true crime. While the crimes vary, the publishing industry has been in a phase where the serial killer seems to be a popular subject.

"But not every crime makes a good book. In a run-of-the-mill crime case, readers won't be fascinated enough to buy a book about it. Unfortunately, a lot of the news these days is really bad and very overwhelming to most people. The tabloidization of America has made people somewhat callused to crime news unless it's really something spectacular. These days it has to be something out of the ordinary that gets our attention, like the Susan Smith case, or a serial murderer like Ted Bundy. Often what makes a crime suitable for a book rather than a news or feature article is probably the sheer bizarreness of the act, the notoriety of the participants, and, in the best cases, the classic overtones of tragedy that reveal a greater truth about the people involved. In that respect, reading true crime is sort of like watching a car wreck—it's fascinating and repellent, but you can't stop watching it. That's why a lot of these books have pictures, which are often really lurid. They draw readers in and it adds a level of authenticity to the story.

"True crime publishing is fairly straightforward since most of the books are mass market paperback originals, but the time constraints on the subject matter are very tight. Most publishers want to get it to market quickly while the case is still strong in the public's mind. So with something like the Heaven's Gate computer cult mass suicide, you'll see a proposal right away. As an editor on books like these, I'm looking for a crime that is newsworthy and a writer who has reporting credentials and/or previous book experience. Publishers are looking for a marketing angle as well as a well-written book. The angle could be the person's credentials, access to the information, or a completely new approach that no one else has come up with or can offer. This makes it tough for a newcomer because, in most cases, they don't have access or the credentials that an editor is looking for.

"When I get a proposal from an agent I review it, and if I don't like it, I reject it. If I like it, I get a second read and we discuss the project in an editorial meeting and ask the basic questions: Is there a book here? And can the author write? It can be a great idea, but if the author can't write then that's all it is—a good idea. If the answers are all 'yes,' then we have to ask 'is this the kind of book we want to publish?' Then there's the issue of the value-added components: Do we have a previously published author? Are there media contacts? Can they support the book? This makes it hard for new or unpublished writers to break in because the publishing industry is becoming risk-averse, much like the movie industry has, because people like to see a sure bet. Then we run the numbers—how many can we sell, how large a book will it be, what will it cost to print? What's the advance? What will it cost to promote? What about the expenses of an author's tour and setting up interviews? If it all looks good, then I call the agent, make an offer, strike a deal, and then cross my fingers and hope the writer puts out a good book.

"I believe that true crime writers are really no different than other writers. Perhaps an eye for detail is important, but being able to produce prose that sparkles, really presents the story well, and offers insights into human nature and the events that they are writing about. When I'm considering a new writer, I look at whether this person can write prose that keeps me interested in the story because I see lots of good ideas but terrible execution.

What all writers owe to themselves and the people who may publish them is to learn how to set up a plot and tell a story because without that you won't succeed. My advice is to read. Read a lot. Take notes. Dissect stories. See what works. Write a journal—the act of writing is like anything else in that the more you do it, the better you get. Don't get discouraged. That's so important. Authors can write six novels and then sell the seventh. But there's probably a reason that the first six didn't sell. What most people don't realize is that many writers can't make a living off their writing. They have a day job and write on the side. But it eventually works out for those that work their butts off and stay with it. No one is a real overnight success, you have to learn the craft and keep at it and not get discouraged."

Michaela Hamilton

Senior Editor, Putnam/Penguin

Hamilton has always been a fan of nonfiction narrative, but her enthusiasm for true crime stories began when she read *Helter Skelter*. Although that was years before she worked in the genre, the appeal of stories that revealed the good and the evil in human nature captivated her as a reader and later as an editor. Less attracted to stories that are filled with bloody details, she prefers cases that help readers increase their understanding of other people and how their minds and motivations work. Hamilton edits between ten and twelve true crime books a year and some of her recent projects have included Ann Rule's *Small Sacrifices*, Jerry Bledsoe's *Bitter Blood, Blood Games,* and *Before He Wakes,* Charles Bosworth Jr.'s *Precious Victims,* and a reprint of Joe McGinness's classic *Fatal Vision* in paperback.

* * * * *

"I think that true crime is a genre that is blurred around the edges. A lot of the best nonfiction narrative goes into true crime because the public pays attention to it and buys it because the shock value draws them in. Generally speaking, the crimes that are written about are really unthinkable. After all, how can a mother kill her children or how can a couple that has been together for years let their relationship degenerate into murder? So while there is always a news value about the circumstances of the murder that's intrinsic in these stories, there's also something more—a bigger theme that deals with societal issues. True crime is more than the combination of a victim, a villain, and a setting. There's got to be a hero, too. Someone the reader can root for who represents the best interests of society. So readers want the shock value of the crime as well as some evidence that the system really works and that the world still makes sense in spite of these horrible people. But I also believe that true crime is instructive because normal people always have a desire to understand the abnormal. People are surrounded by violence these days and they are looking for a way to understand it. In that sense, true crime stories serve a cautionary purpose because they carry a subtle warning that people should be careful and take precautions even in the most normal of circumstances and settings. That they should heed all those simple warnings about who they open the door to or where they park the car or that they should leave lights on. True crime offers the public its right to know about crime, about how these things happen, about what drives people to do these things, and that the justice system works. That's why it has always been a popular genre, not because it provides sick kicks.

"I think it is important to note that the market for books has dwindled in general because of media overload and true crime has been impacted by that. After all, these days you can read about crime everywhere or see it on a television show any night of the week. There are a hundred venues for people to get information from and, as publishers, we have to be grateful that there are still people who like to get it from books. But one of the big problems with a book in this environment is timeliness. Headlines capture a lot of attention and scrutiny, but by the time we can publish a book, it's not news any more and so it has to offer something else, something new. The true crime writer has to be able to offer something beyond the headlines. That's what I look for and that's what a reader looks for in a book. It can't be a cut-and-paste job like an insta-book because there has to be a level of depth and complexity or a completely new angle that no one has been able to bring to the coverage before. As an editor, the first thing I look for is a really good writer who has a solid story with a lot of twists. The good stories are always those with a string of surprising developments and a bunch of really interesting people and social issues. The best are ones that illuminate important societal issues—incest, child abuse, family dynamics—in a way that hasn't been seen before. I've found that when there's a real issue involved, a good writer can really do something of lasting social importance in a book that makes it different from all of the coverage that has preceded it.

"Most of my submissions are from agents, but sometimes I get a query from a journalist who has been covering the story. This is a tough area for new writers to break into because of the skills involved. You have to be able to research a story and tell a good narrative and it's a tougher combination to find than you might think. What people don't realize is that these are not easy books to write. Badly executed true crime books tend to be very repetitious: You have the crime, somebody discovers it, the investigation follows the trail of the killer, the trial, the penalty phase, and so on. It's a challenge for the writer to structure it in a way that is not boring, one that skillfully releases the information. I need writers who can do research and do narrative writing and that's tough because journalists can do the research but often can't develop a narrative. That's because writing a four-thousand-word story is different from a ninety-thousand-word book. While I often have to give them really detailed editorial guidance, I've found that novelists who are crossing over are just the opposite. They know a good story, but don't know how to do the research, work with sources, or get people to open up in an interview.

"Unlike other editors, I don't use gory photos in our inserts. The worst might be a body in a body bag being carried out because, at their heart, true crime stories are human interest stories. As a result, I tend to use people and place photos to capture the characters and the setting. If you look at *Fatal Vision* you will see that it was released as a hard cover with no photos because it was aimed at an upper-class audience and it was felt that it wouldn't enhance the appeal. But we added a photo insert when we did the paperback reprint because we thought that the end of the market would respond to it.

Despite these differences, I think it's important to understand that there is no longer a serious hardcover market for true crime any more. There's simply too much competition at a lower price point and people don't need to spend $25 for a book when they can get something like it for $5. From a publisher's perspective, a hard cover will take an extra year and more money to produce while you can get a paperback to market quicker. That just makes the story a year older and then it has to compete with newer stories, making it more difficult to sell. But it's just not a publisher's decision anymore. It depends on book buyers and what they want, because they really drive the business these days. Booksellers all have sophisticated computer systems to monitor sales and then they buy accordingly, so we're not alone in the decision about what to publish. That's changed the market for true crime and everything else."

Jessica Lichenstein

Senior Editor, HarperCollins, New York

Lichenstein started editing true crime while working as an editor at Signet. Signet was one of the leading publishers of the genre's paperback editions, so she gained a great deal of experience in a short time. When she moved on to HarperCollins her track record made her a natural choice for editing any new true crime acquisitions. Less fascinated with the more lurid tales based on "body counts" than with those that reveal that "truth is stranger than fiction," Lichenstein tends to focus on the moment when that strange line is crossed from normality into depravity. Like every aficionado, she is fascinated by the simple yet often unanswered question that is at the core of every true crime reader's mind: "what causes people to do that?"

* * * * *

"What sets true crime apart is the 'ordinariness' of the people involved. You read these books and continually ask yourself 'how did they get that way?' and 'why did they do that?' because it's always extreme behavior in every case. But often the causes that drive these acts are very commonplace—divorce, greed, adultery, kids gone wrong—the sort of things you see in everyday life. That's what's so interesting to me. On one hand, you have motivating factors that are often not all that uncommon, but which drive people to these exceptionally perverse acts. The gap between the two can offer a window into a side of human nature that reveals what pushes people over the edge. That's why books that feature 'the boy next door type' always attract so much attention. Because it makes people look up from the book and think twice about their neighbor and how close—or how far—they are from this type of terror. Most people believe that there are places in the world that are safe and others that are unsafe and many successful true crime books are placed in places that seem to be very safe, places like Wisconsin or Kansas, and this shakes that worldview and draws readers in. For the reader, it's sort of a sensation of 'there but for the grace of God go I,' and it's a feeling that fascinates them—that unanswered question about what pushes people to those extremes. On the other hand, I believe that the purely sensational aspect of true crime writing has worn thin with the reading public. Police computer techniques have made tracking serial killers easier, so there seem to be fewer and fewer of the great manhunts as material and the tabloids have made the bizarre commonplace.

"There are really just two ways to do true crime now, either as a quick 'insta-book' in paperback or a bigger, more serious book that merits a hard cover. The market has changed in this regard because, in the past, true crime could go either way. But the audience has shifted and media pressure has heightened the awareness of cases that once would have made good books. Now, after reading the paper and watching the news and newsmagazines, people often feel that they 'know everything' about a case and won't buy a book. Most of the successful true crime books start out as hardbacks and then go to the softback market. These are typically bigger projects from name authors who have a proven appeal because a true crime book has to be special to make it as a hardback these days. In terms of our paperback books, what HarperCollins has been employing is a 'tie-in' approach with the *New York Post*. [Both are part of Rupert Murdoch's media conglomerate.] If the case is time sensitive, we will often take the *Post* writer who has been covering it and have them do a paperback original. Then the *Post* will promote it through serialization or advertisements and we will mutually support the project to make it successful. But the story always has to be strong to merit committing to any type of book and it's not enough to have a basic crime or even a serial killer as a subject. In most cases, the crime is probably more suited to a magazine article, especially if there isn't a larger message contained in the story. To do a book, there has to be something universal that speaks to people who would never do something like this, something in the background that addresses a larger, more common, human condition that adds a dimension. This is one of the two things I look at right away, the other being how resolved the case is.

"Personally, I'm looking for very little in the true crime area because right now there's not much that is suitable for a paperback market because of the media coverage of unusual crimes. And I'm not looking for unagented material. Agents tend to represent material with more leeway in terms of time and we look at the merits of the book. No matter the genre, I'm drawn to characters and I look for a strong sense of people rather than a 'body count.' I also look at whether or not the story holds up on a psychological level—does it hold together and read well? Unlike some other editors working in this area, I'm not interested in a Jeffery Dahlmer type of experience which is so far outside most people's reality that it might as well be fiction. Other than the characters, I look for the specifics of the crime and whether the case has been resolved or not. I like a crime that is wrapped up whether or not someone has been convicted. With a book about a case where there hasn't been a conviction, we typically do a heavy legal review with our legal department to insulate ourselves from any potential lawsuits. In telling the tale, the writer often unwittingly implicates other people who may indeed be innocent and thus libeled. I look for things like this right away. I prefer to work with finished cases because it makes this part easier and then you don't wait for cases to be resolved so you can schedule the book's publication. That way you don't have to question the ultimate ending.

"On the whole, I'm very selective in this area because this is a tough genre to break into. There's a lot of competition from other genres—legal thrillers, mysteries, suspense—and there's simply more books out there that have a lot of the factual elements that people have traditionally looked to true crime to supply. I don't meet readers who say 'I only read true crime' like they might say 'I love cozy little mysteries.' People like true crime because of the juicy information about subjects they only know a little about, such as autopsies, investigative techniques, murder scene details, or to find out how cops really work. But now those elements can be found in other formats and that's probably draining readers off.

"I think that there is a growing link between the basics of true crime and other genres that have cut down on its popularity over the last few years. Lots of modern mysteries such as *The Alienist* have slowly siphoned off sales because they use so much more factual information to color the setting. That draws off readers who had always turned to true crime to get that type of writing—narratives filled with revealing, factual tidbits about history, forensics, police work, and so forth. In fact, many early converts to true crime writing were converts from the mystery genre. They loved the mystery part, but the

273

fact that the events and people were all real added another dimension to it that fiction couldn't provide. But now there's a lot of that in the market in other genres and it's slowed down true crime sales. But it's important to remember that things go in cycles when it comes to sales—legal thrillers, mystery, and true crime—and everything comes back eventually. Despite the decline in true crime sales in general, historical true crime is quite popular and I think it's an exciting time for writers because there's more latitude as a result of this crossover between genres. There's more opportunity out there for writers."

Mary Ann Lynch

Senior Editor, Macmillan Books, New York

Unlike other editors, the decision to edit true crime projects was a personal one for Lynch. Fascinated with societal trends, human behavior, and stories that offered a compelling read, Lynch found true crime "an intersection where facts meet an incredibly dramatic story." Although Macmillan does not have a dedicated imprint for true crime, Lynch handles all of the publisher's books in the genre. As a result, she's the person who will be contacted by everyone from detectives to psychics taking part in major criminal investigations. Recent projects have included Donald Freed's *Killing Time,* Charles Whitlock's *Whitlock's Scam School,* and Doreen Orion's *I Know You Really Love Me.*

* * * * *

"I think that there's a real opening in the market for books that are true but that teach you about criminals and their activities. They're instructive in many ways, but you also get the drama of crime. As a rule, criminals are nothing more than people who do things very well and readers are always fascinated with that. The criminal mind is a peculiar form of genius and what appeals to people is that aspect of 'how did they do it?' Criminals are often sophisticated and their crimes usually take a great deal of intelligence and thought, both qualities that reveal a great deal about people. Besides, their approach is usually one that most honest, law-abiding people would have never considered. The best true crime books always have those elements in them and they often crystallize problems that exist on a larger level in our society. But the media have changed true crime in ways that go beyond the speed and flow with which information reaches the public. Since we live in an era where we are involved in unfolding events via direct feeds from the news media, readers have become much more sophisticated in what they look for in true crime writing. People now usually have the facts before they sit down to read something so they are looking for the analysis behind it and how it all fits together. True crime can go beyond the facts and reveal all of that in a way that the tight format of the modern electronic media can't deliver.

"As an editor, I want to do books that are important and contribute. A well-done true crime book can provide a certain depth and texture in telling a story—something that is gripping, dramatic, and instructive—that is a hard combination to find in other genres. Just as a novel tells us about ourselves through the thoughts and actions of others in a created world, true crime does that like nothing else in the real world while allowing people to venture into the dark side of humanity in a safe manner. A lot of people in the publishing industry say that true crime's time has passed, but I think they are absolutely wrong. It is simply that the market has shifted a bit and we need a new way to frame it.

"True crime interests readers because it deals with subjects that we are surrounded by—crime and violence. Once you take a crime and put it into a different format—a book—it becomes something else. We're always fascinated with a story, whether a love story or a crime story, when it deals with basic elements of the human condition and people are always drawn to that. We're always aware that we are connected to not only the angels but the demons as well and in modern society it's hard to walk closer to the angels every day. True crime is helpful by being instructive in this regard. I don't think that you can be streetwise enough these days and we get an education from these types of books because they tell us things we don't already know. That's something different from any other genre.

"When I consider a project, I always ask 'Is it something that I haven't read before?' or 'Does it take me someplace new?' I'm the kind of editor that is willing to look at something new or that has potential, but will take a lot of work. I'm willing to work with people, which is unusual in this business, but that's how you come up with something new and different. When I see a proposal, I'm already thinking about the jacket copy in my head. I like to think of the total package when I first get it because to sell a book you have to figure out who wants to buy it. A lot of first books from major publishing houses will average a seventy-five hundred or ten-thousand print run, which is in the realm of a small press but they have such a large overhead that cuts into the promotability of the book. Positioning and getting people interested in it are key factors in bringing any book to market and you have to look at those issues right from the start.

"I've found that a big pitfall with a lot of true crime writers is predictability. If you can read the first page and see what's going to happen—to anticipate it—you're in trouble because it's formulaic and there's no subtlety. That's the key to good crime writing, to be able to do incredible research and immerse yourself in it to the point where you dream about it. In the best examples of the genre, people are immersed and so involved that the other world is yours and that carries onto the page. That's what people want—to be taken into another world and learn about it—and the unsuccessful books are those that are formulaic and flat and don't involve the reader. The best true crime writing has a pulse that takes you with it and carries you away into another world and that's what I look for when considering a project. True crime does what criminals do—it seduces you into believing and not wanting to walk away even though you know something horrible will happen."

Betty Prashker

Senior Editor, Crown Books, New York

A legendary editor who has worked successfully in all areas of publishing, Prashker has edited a number of true crime books over the last three decades. These have included everything from classic works such as Tommy Thompson's *Blood and Money* to more recent efforts by Dominick Dunne. While she continues to work in many areas, Prashker has seen the nature of the modern true crime genre change over the years.

* * * * *

"Both the market for true crime and the type of books that define the genre have changed dramatically in the last ten to fifteen years. Capote started the popularity of modern true crime writing with *In Cold Blood* in the 1960s and then Tommy Thompson's *Blood and Money* came along and built upon that. These were followed by other classics such as Vincent Bugliosi's *Helter Skelter* and Joe McGinness's *Fatal Vision* and, in my opinion, the 1970s were the golden age of true crime writing. Since then, it has not been as popular on the high end of the market. Although true crime has seen a big growth in the area of paperbacks, there are fewer books that are in the Capote class in terms of the writing or literary merit. Now we've switched into true law rather than true crime. If you consider the O.J. Simpson case, you'll see that we've had sixty-three-plus books, many of which have been on the bestseller list despite the number of people who say they've had enough of it, that they're sick of it. But all of these books deal with the legal system rather than the crime or the criminal element and that is a significant change.

"The one thing that hasn't changed is that people are always fascinated by crime in high places. In the Simpson case there was a sports star icon, his blond wife, sex, wealth, glamour, and crime. That's what people love to read about, not an everyday shooting or robbery. To be successful, a true crime book has to be about people who are larger than life. Just consider *Midnight in the Garden of Evil* as an example. It was on the bestseller list for two years because it had everything—sex, wealth, charisma, the works—as opposed to the story of some guy who had an antique shop on 14th Street and was shot during a robbery. Yes, that case is interesting to his family, friends, and neighbors, but not to the reading public. It isn't complex or compelling enough and the people involved are quite ordinary. A lot of the appeal of true crime comes down to human nature, and while I think that people are always interested in crime, who commits it, and how it is solved, they are more interested if the characters or settings are glamorous. Part of this comes from the tabloidization of television. Overexposure has taken a lot of appeal and excitement out of the core of the true crime market and the quickie paperback books also have taken a bite out of it. Now everyone knows all the lurid details about the latest case as soon as they are uncovered. These days, the true crime books that really work are the ones that bring another dimension to it, that tell a story in a way that goes beyond reporting 'this is what happened.' Often, it is through the viewpoint of writers who can take their insights into a crime and the circumstances around it and make it into a rich and textured experience for the reader rather than a bald recitation of lurid or violent events.

"I look for that extra dimension in a project. Any crime that attracts enough attention to generate a book proposal will wind up having several books written about it, so you really need to have a writer who can bring something special to the case beyond reporting skills. But it varies from writer to writer and case to case. Take some of the current high-profile crime cases in the news as examples. The JonBenet Ramsey case? In my opinion, there's no real story there. The recent murder of Jonathan Levin [the son of Time-Warner's CEO who was robbed and murdered in his New York City apartment] was nothing more than an unfortunate robbery and murder that, while tragic, does not carry a story people want to read about. On the other hand, the Alex Kelly rape case might have something because of the mix of elements involved. I don't know if anything will come of it, but the elements are certainly there. You have the drug culture in an affluent high school, his parents' status as nouveau riche in New England's old money culture, the closed-mouthed community of Darien, the extended time he spent hiding from the authorities, the flash of the European resorts he stayed at while on the run, the European girlfriend versus the American girlfriend who waited for him and stood by him during the trial, it's quite a mix. But each publishing house varies in what they want to print, so there is a lot of opportunity for writers, but that doesn't always translate into a lot of good books. Essentially, the market for true crime is wide if shallow at the moment. Personally, I pick what appeals to me and what I think will sell. The glamour, a sense of the larger world, the money, and the sex, those are the ingredients I look for in a proposal."

Charles Spicer

Senior Editor, St. Martin's Press, New York

Spicer has edited a healthy list of the genre's bestsellers at both ends of the literary spectrum. He worked on commercial fiction at Delacorte/Dell before moving on to St. Martin's, the publishing house the *New York Times* has called "the leader in true crime." Noting that a steady diet of murder stories is "pretty grim stuff to do all the time," Spicer has expanded his nonfiction repertoire to a wide range of other areas. He has recently completed projects as diverse as *The Renaissance,* a Stephen Koontz thriller, and an autobiography of Joan Collins. In addition, he edits between twelve and fifteen true crime books each year.

* * * * *

"I really believe that true crime has to have a murder in it someplace. There has to be a body and the kinkier, the weirder, the stranger, the more twisted the motivation behind the murder, the more fascinating the case. Readers are fascinated by the extremes of human character and by real-life drama and the sense that it could have happened to them.

"That's why true crime has always been popular. But there are more ways to get a story out now and people learn about crimes through newspapers, the tabloids,

People magazine, the evening news, television news-magazines and movies, and paperbacks. The interest has always been there, but now it is just being exploited in many different formats and that's altered the way publishers look at the genre. Media exposure has changed everything, but the media also drive the public's attention and appetite at a speed that is not well suited to the traditional pace of publishing. Sometimes that pressure forces our decision on whether to pass on a book or to do it as an instant paperback. We've done a lot of insta-books and have come to dominate the market in that area. Our books on the Susan Smith case and the Jeffery Dahlmer case were bestsellers. The thing about them is that is they are produced with the speed of a magazine but provide the depth and detail that a magazine can't deliver. I know people put these types of books down, but I don't think they have looked at some of the better ones out there. We use seasoned journalists who are used to writing for deadline and that makes a big difference in a highly competitive marketplace.

"Like every editor, I talk to agents all the time. But I also get story ideas for projects from all sorts of sources and I'm willing to look at everything. I have a file I keep for possible ideas and, in cases where I find a story, I'll approach one of the writers I work with on a regular basis and see if they're interested in the project. Writers also come to me all the time because they know I'm looking for stories with a sensational nature or a fresh twist to something. Right now, we have a number of paperbacks coming out that all have a similar angle. Fred Rosen came to me with *Gang Mom,* the story of a mother who's opposed to gangs in her neighborhood but was found to be their biggest supporter behind the scenes, and Sannie Weinstein and Melinda Wilson's *Buried Bodies* about a very successful businessman in Indiana who had secret gay life. Whenever his family was out of town he would bring guys back to his house, have sex, and then kill them and bury them in the yard. What works in all these books is the issue of secret lives, that the upstanding neighbor next door is really up to something you would never believe.

"What I look at when deciding on a project comes down to several basic questions. The first is 'Is this case an interesting one?' Then it's 'What are the writer's credentials?' The writer's background is important because there's a big difference between writing an article and doing a book. In a book you have to be able to create characters and the full narrative of a story; it's not about just being able to report the facts. But not everyone can do it. Every newspaper reporter can deliver the facts in a coherent manner, but I always have to ask whether they can tell a story. So I look at a writer's track record before I'll commit to a project. I have used writers new to the genre, but I like to see several test chapters to make sure. I also like to see existing news clips about the case to see how it was covered. Beyond the crime and the characters involved, the other thing I always look at is 'What is the setting?' Is it interesting and can the writer link the crime to the setting in a way that is revealing and compelling for readers? Then come the photographs. Photos are important in true crime because it sets the genre apart. This is particularly important in the paperback market where the bottom line on photos is 'gross is great.'

"Marketwise, trade hardcover is very difficult for true crime because there's so much competition from quickly produced paperbacks and television movies out there. It's very hard to break into the hardcover market unless you have an existing track record and even the big names have seen their sales drop over the last few years. Paperback is the market for true crime because of the price range and the belief that much of this writing is viewed as entertainment by readers. But the good news is that paperback sales are very steady in true crime. I keep hearing people say that it's collapsed because some houses have overpublished the genre, but true crime is one of our most solid markets."

Chapter Ten

CRIME ON CAMERA

When Hollywood Comes Calling

Whether a feature film or a network movie of the week, Hollywood has always depended on adapting true stories when it comes to the search for fresh material. Part of the appeal is the same as it is in publishing: Crime stories that would be considered unbelievable or trite as fiction draw attention and a solid share of the viewing audience simply because they are based in reality. Plus the growing media emphasis on lurid crimes offers studios and networks extensive free publicity and help to make a film stand out from the rest of the competition.

But the needs of the film and television industries are very different when it comes to how a story is told. Many successful nonfiction writers have come to loathe

the treatment their work receives once it has been adapted to a different medium. Some, lured by the perception of glamour and tales of big money, are quick to try their hand at turning the truth into drama—only to learn that their skills don't translate. Others find that their roles as "consultants" in the development phase of a project mean little more than an extra paycheck. Few ever find the experience a happy one and most who have tried it once are quick to sell off the rights to a project and start work on their next book.

So what happens in between? As in publishing, the market for true crime stories has changed over the last few years. Budgets are tighter, media overexposure is both a friend and a foe, unique stories seem harder to find, and network, studio, and audience tastes keep changing. While the commitment to telling a tale that entertains and enlightens is shared by most producers and writers, the demands of the medium are unforgiving and the writer must bend before it. Making it in Hollywood is tougher than ever, but it certainly helps if you understand the rules of the game.

Janet Faust-Krusi

Once Upon A Time Productions

After working for nearly twenty years as a producer specializing in adapting true stories for long-format television movies, Faust-Krusi has seen it all. She worked for a variety of major production companies, including NMB, Spectacorp, and Kushner-Locke, before joining forces with Stan Brooks and starting Once Upon A Time in 1996. "Stan and I had been competitors for years, but we decided to join forces while sitting next to each other on a plane while on the way to try and sign up the rights for the same true story and complaining about how tough this business was."

* * * * *

"We're like machines here when it comes to looking for stories. We read everything, all the time—newspapers, books, magazine articles, original stories, everything that might have a story that will work on film. But there are several levels of stories that we're looking for. If it is a big story that has captured the headlines, there's obviously going to be interest because it's essentially presold to the public—everyone is aware of it already. The value of that publicity might be on the scale of a big book because everyone knows about it and people are ready to see it. They want to see what really happened behind the scenes, or to see a particular act or a character that they know about from reading the newspaper. That's great because it makes the show stand out in people's minds. Then there's a second tier of stories, the ones that aren't national and don't have all the attention, but are still dramatic enough to be appealing. People are always interested in things that are true because they think, 'Wow, that could have happened to my neighbor or my relative,' or the fact that someone actually did something horrible or something heroic could be frightening or inspiring to them and they'll be interested enough to watch it. In either case, these stories are morality plays on some level. There is always a character at the center of it that you can root for, someone that goes through a life-altering experience that transforms them. This is directly opposed to a series, where the same character is showing up week after week and not going through a once-in-a-lifetime altering event, something that reinforces the belief that the system really does work or, if the system doesn't work, that people prevail in spite of it.

"The difficulty in true stories, and true crime in particular, is that 99 percent of the true crime stories we see these days are about family members killing family members for money. Those aren't very interesting any more. In many ways, the true crime genre is really constricted now because all the stories have been done in one way or another. It would take a new twist to get our attention and these days it seems to be a lot of the same thing over and over again—a lot of serial murderers or spouses killing spouses. If there is a really great crime story out there, one that gives us something new to look at and think about, that presents a new dilemma, we'd love to see it. So finding a good story is harder now because there's not much that's new. I've been in this business for so long that I hear pitches for stories that are just like a movie I did fifteen years ago. But when you do find a great story in the newspaper, then you get in touch with the person and you sign them to an option. The option is good-faith money based on the fact that you will take their story and be able to sell it to a network. It's essentially an option against the money we will get as a purchase price from the network. People think that they can get rich at this stage, but they don't realize that there's often limited money for an option, especially if you have to option the stories of two or three people to get the whole thing. The budgets for television movies are often smaller than you might think and we want to put every dime on the screen. Then there's not huge profits for a story once it gets made. We typically make a long-format television movie for about $2.7 million for everything, so there's not a lot to go around. After all, you have to handle development expenses, get a script written, pay for all the production costs, and pay for the stars. There's not a lot left over.

"My personal bugaboo with true crime in the long-story television genre is that I really feel that there has to be a level of morality present somewhere in a story. It can't be a celebration of the criminal. There has to be something more, a point of view that contains a morality play that people can learn from. Take one of the first and most important true crime stories in a long form, *Hands of a Stranger*, as an example. It was the story about a friend of Ted Bundy's who knew him very well and was reporting on the story of this terrible serial killer, but never realized that the monster he was writing about was his charismatic friend. Or the Joe McGinniss story that was told through the eyes of the parents who come to realize that their beloved son-in-law killed both their daughter and granddaughter. I believe very strongly that we, as story tellers and producers, have to do a story that has a purpose, that provides something more than just entertainment. If there were consequences of a crime, if people were hurt, then we have to have a point of view that deals with that aspect of the story. It can't be just wanting to get into the killer's mind. What's the point of a story like that? Take *Natural Born Killers*. What's the point of watching people kill other people? Most of the people I know in the industry and the audience say that they are really disgusted with the pointless violence that shows up in the movies these days. People want to be moved emotionally and they want to think about things or be inspired—they really do. There's certainly a lot of violence in our world, but does that mean we need to show it? I believe we have a responsibility to portray the consequences of violence, that the impact is awful and that it's not 'cartoon violence' where a character gets squashed and then they pop right back up. People need to understand that violent crimes ruin people's lives, that loved ones are left behind and that it is awful.

"From a producer's standpoint, true stories are extremely hard to put together. It's tough to get all the rights and you need the right point of view to make it work. Then, once you have the cooperation of the people involved, you have a huge responsibility to them to make the story right and have them like it. On top of that, you have an obligation to the network and the people involved on that level. We have to hand in a very detailed script to the network's legal department to be vetted and we have to stay pretty true to the original story for legal reasons. That may not sound like a challenge, but there is a difficulty in turning something from real life into a dramatic story that works on television. In some ways, it's more difficult than starting from scratch because you have to be accountable to the network, to the people whose story it is, and to your own attorneys so that you don't get a lawsuit once the show airs. All these elements have to be factored in whenever you're developing a project.

"When it comes to adapting a project, the interesting thing is that neither a three-act structure or a seven-act structure really impacts how the story is told. A three-act adaptation for a feature film will have all the same moves that a television movie does. In a seven-act television movie, it has to grab the audience within the first five or ten minutes so they have an idea of what's going to happen, but aren't quite sure of how it will be resolved. In terms of the script, by the end of the first act—right around page twenty-three—you have your first big twist in the plot. By the third act, right at the commercial break at the top of the hour, you have to set the themes for the second hour's action. That happens somewhere between pages fifty and fifty-five in the script. By that point, you've got your characters, you've got your plot basics, a major plot twist, and now you get a major event to keep the audience tuned in for the second hour. You've got to capture their attention with something so it's not just 'fill in the blanks' for the second half. If you do that, you'll lose them. They'll just change the channel because they already can figure out what's going to happen next. But now the networks are looking for more of a 'grabber' on the opening and that forces you to move the action up, which can create problems in the second half.

"The biggest problem with an adaptation is to find a story with an active central character because in most true stories the central character is not overtly active. In life, most people go through an emotional journey that is reactive to outside events and that journey is internal. But for film you need a character who is active because everything happens through action and dialogue. The other issue is that real life rarely fits neatly into a seven-act structure. An event or a transformation of a character might have taken place over twenty-four hours or ten years. It never happens in two hours. So you have to compress or expand time while remaining true to the dynamics of the story. That's what a lot of people don't understand, especially the people whose story is being adapted. For example, I was doing a story about an Olympic skater and the actress who was playing her was wearing white skates for a scene. The person—the real skater—was on the set watching and went nuts about the fact that she had really been wearing beige skates. I tried to point out that the issue was to keep the story true to the emotional reality, the interactions, and the chronology of events so the essence of the emotional journey she experienced remained intact. Sure we compress timelines or condense people to make it fit in a two-hour format, but we keep all the relationships, emotions, and events and their impact intact to capture the spirit of what really happened. But that wasn't the point for her. It was having beige skates—something that no viewer would ever notice. So we wound up stopping the production and finding beige skates."

Michael Jaffe

Jaffe-Braunstein Productions

Jaffe was literally born into the television business. His father was a pioneering producer who did NBC's legendary *Producer's Showcase* in the 1950s, the original *Peter Pan* movie, and more than four hundred Dinah Shore shows. Jaffe started to work for his father while he was doing Shore's talk show and eventually began to sell and produce programs on his own. He and his partner Howard Braunstein specialize exclusively in developing movies and miniseries based on true stories for cable, broadcast, and network programming. "I'm interested in true stories because they're the only thing a small independent producer can still own and sell."

* * * * *

"The market for these stories is strong. The major networks have been consuming over a hundred movies a year since the late sixties. That's enormous and it's grown as new broadcast outlets have appeared. Now there's Turner, Lifetime, HBO, the Family Channel, and USA looking for material, so that's up to nearly two hundred movies a year. As a producer, you have to look somewhere for those stories and that's where real-life dramas or crimes come in. No matter what people say, there aren't two hundred books or two hundred great original concepts out there each year, so you've got to look in the newspapers, the magazines, or the nightly news for material. Besides, it's what people are fascinated with. Take a look at the Amy Fisher story. Two networks, ABC and NBC, got thirty shares with their movies about that case. Those are huge figures. Then CBS got a twenty-four share with its movie. So you have three movies about the same crime and people still tuned in to watch them. People are crazy to learn about the details about someone else's extraordinary life or experience. I suppose it might be endemic to the species, that it's just part of human nature that we're just interested in the lives of other people. Take a look at the success of magazines like *People, US,* or the *Star* or the *Globe.* The networks are keenly aware of this and when you can find a good true story, they love it because they know people will watch. The fascination with someone else's life is everywhere.

I've lived in small towns of all sizes and the appetite for this kind of information is always there. We all love a dramatic story with a beginning, a middle, and an end and if there's all sorts of twists or a crime involved, so much the better.

"But in spite of this fascination and the growing demand for movies, it's still a tough business. I would estimate that the success ratio is around two or three to one in terms of projects that are optioned and sold to a network and those that actually get made. Naturally, if you have a track record and you're successful, you'll do better. If not or if you're new to the industry, you'll do worse. Like any business, it is all based on relationships and that complicates it for someone who's just coming up. But no matter who you are, it is still tough to find a good true story that will work. If it is a breaking news story and there's heat around it, the network already knows about it and other producers will be involved right from the start. The competition is very tough and you have to be extremely aggressive. Sometimes that means spending a lot of money up front, money that you're gambling on making back. When the Amy Fisher case broke, my partner Howard flew out to Long Island and visited with the Buttafucos. But all they wanted to offer were the rights to a bad story, a whitewash of what really happened that made them look good rather than what really happened. The story was all over the papers, so who was going believe a version like that? So we decided to go with Amy Fisher's version. We went to a writer who had done an insta-book on the case and we optioned that. In the meantime, there were two guys who got the rights to her story in exchange for arranging her bail. We waited for the court to approve that deal and then we optioned their rights so we could interview her and combined the stories. But that's often what it takes just to get the right to make a movie. Sometimes you have to fly right out to the location and offer a lot of money to tie up the person's story even though you haven't sold it to anyone yet.

"It may sound funny, but the truth is the tail wags the dog in television. The natural arc to the 'perfect television story' is one that the networks love. There is no natural arc. We develop projects to meet their needs and those needs change from year to year. This just reflects changes in the market and the needs of the networks to respond to those changes. That means that true crime stories can be hot one year and then give way to historical stories or family dramas the next. A lot of it is timing because everything goes in cycles. But the basic criterion is that a good story has characters that you can sympathize with who are going through interesting events that are changing their lives. Once you have a story like that, you just have to figure out how to make it in a cost-effective manner. In the feature business, most people go out and budget scripts and that can take months. We don't, we script budgets. We start with the premise that it can only cost so much, because if it costs more than that we don't make a profit. When it comes to adapting a story to a normal two-hour script, I'll read it, make some notes, take out a pro forma budget we use, make a few adjustments from the last project we made, and—bam—I have a budget. It takes about twenty minutes at the most. This is the opposite of the feature business where it can take at least five months to get a budget together and approved by the studios.

"We almost never use an original writer on a project, someone who has written a book about a case. Every production company has writers that they work with all the time. I have about five that I use for adaptations and they're the essence of the business. They all follow the same format because all the networks want to take you pretty close to the half-hour break in the first act. Then the hour break has to be strong so the audience doesn't switch over to sitcom. Then the breaks between acts get closer and closer together the further in you get into the story to keep the pace going and the audience tuned in. The breaks between the final acts are only about seven to eight minutes apart. At the end of the day in this market, you won't see many movies that say 'Based on a true story,' They will say 'Inspired by real events' or 'Based on real events' or something like that because by the time you wind up compositing characters and filling in dramatic gaps, that's what you have. Plus there are the Standards and Practices rules to adhere to and corporate policy issues dominate over all else. One network developed a true story about a union of prostitutes, but it didn't get made because the corporate policy was that they wouldn't make a movie about a prostitute who was a nice person or a hero to others. They care about their sponsors and critics who might be able to accuse or malign them in any way, shape, or form. That makes it tough to satisfy their needs and almost impossible to tell a true story any more."

Frank von Zurnick

Von Zurnick-Sutner Productions

Von Zurnick has made over a hundred movies over the course of the last twenty years, the majority of which have been *event-based*—industry jargon for true stories based on real crimes or historic events. He has adapted several of Edna Buchanan's true crime books and worked with literary luminaries such as Gore Vidal on other projects. His company makes both movies of the week and miniseries for clients such as ABC, CBS, NBC, Fox, Showtime, and Disney. "I love true stories because they're stranger than fiction."

* * * * *

"Television is wonderful for a producer because of the endless appetite for material. I used to work in the theater and produce plays and I loved to work with writers, but there was no money in it. The networks are always looking for that kind of talent, so it was pretty easy to break in when I started. I've done a lot of projects over the years and although I'm not an ambulance chaser, I know that true stories are popular because the audience marvels at the incredible plot twists rather than wondering 'who made this up?' The networks know that too. The business looks for true stories because they do better for a variety of reasons. If a film is based on a real person's story, then they get to do the talk show circuit, sometimes with the actor who plays them, and that's extra publicity for the show. Plus the audience hears about or sees advertisements for between a hundred twenty-five and a hundred fifty films each year and if they remember the story because it's true, it helps break through the media clutter. If they recall it, it sells it better and some of the events are so astonishing that they make great drama—especially when there's a crime involved.

"I look for material in three places: headlines, history, and the judicial system. The headlines are an obvious place to start, but everyone else is reading them too, so there's a lot of competition. Nonfiction historical books are often quite good and they are big with Turner, especially for things like Native American history. In the case of justice, there's crimes, but there's often a very fertile arena for issues of injustice because we can look back at certain events and can see that the participants were judged unfairly at the time. In all of these, you always search for a theme or a point of view or an ethical premise that is bigger than the action itself. A perfect story is something that demonstrates ordinary people in extraordinary circumstances, people who buck the system and are ultimately proven right, people with courage. That's what audiences ultimately respond to. They like the drama, but it's the characters and their struggles that offer the appeal.

"But adapting true stories to television has its own problems because television operates on a seven-act structure, one that is filled with interruptions. So by the end of act one, about twenty-five minutes into the hour, you have to have the theme out there and establish what the essential conflict is. By the third act, which should come right at the ten o'clock hour where the viewer has the chance to change the channel, you have to have a plot turn that drives the second hour of the movie right to the end. Feature films are different because the audience is a prisoner so you can wait until the end of the second act or into the third before turning up the heat.

"The biggest challenge when adapting is not to inject your own subjective viewpoints about the story. When this happens it can often be to the detriment of what really happened. We usually have to compress timelines and characters to maintain the dramatic pace required by the format, but the point of view has to be really balanced to make it work. That's one of the reasons we use writers who specialize in adaptations.

"When it comes to adapting a book into a script, I would say that nine times out of ten we use the author as a consultant. They can really help in keeping things balanced and preventing diversions from reality because they've done all the leg work, all the research, and know the story cold. The only catch is that they have to understand that it is a different format. Part of the problem is that a writer produces a 'child' when they write a book. They often have three years into the thing and it's very hard to let go and see it go into another medium. Actors address things differently, the pace is different, the director has nuances that change the way things come across and that's different for writers. They see it as what it was and the change is sometimes difficult to accept, particularly for journalists and sometimes even novelists. They see it one way and it comes out another. I also won't deny that there are people in my field who are more sensationalistic than we are in their approach, and that has an impact on the way some things come out. But once we have a script, that's usually it. Small changes can take place during the course of a production, but the script that the network has approved is the bible when shooting. After all, it's not like a light goes on the tenth day of shooting, and you suddenly realize how it ought to be done. Once you have a script that works and it's approved, you follow it all the way through. At that point, it's come down to just getting the damn thing made."

Shannon Richardson

Writer/Producer

A former policewoman turned writer who uncovered extensive corruption in the Texas jail systems, Richardson represents a growing element in Hollywood—the writer/producer. As an independent, she works both ends of a deal to get her stories on the screen. But the difference is that Richardson exclusively deals with adapting true stories, many of which are based on crimes. She currently has twenty-five projects in development and has written five books. "True stories go right to people's emotions, they provide something that an audience can personally identify with."

* * * * *

"I started working in the realm of true stories out of self-defense. When I was real new to the industry, I had an agent who sent me out to a high-powered producer who was looking for a star vehicle on television. I had a story that was perfect and I pitched it, but got turned down. Naturally, I was disappointed, but things come and go and I forgot all about it. Then a year later I saw a television program featuring the star that was exactly the same as the concept I had pitched, but the characters had different names. I went to an attorney, but this was before the Art Buchwald case had set a standard about stealing someone else's concepts. He told me that I had a pretty solid case, but I should really think about pressing charges because I would lose either way. Basically, if I won I would lose because no one would ever work with me. So I started to think about how I could protect myself and I realized that true stories were the way to go because no one could steal it from me. Well, they can steal the idea or the title, but it makes it really difficult. Then I found that it had an added bonus. Like a lot of writers, I was always shy about pitching my own stuff. But I really enjoyed pitching someone else's story and I could do it with more enthusiasm and energy than I could muster for my own original work. I also discovered that I enjoyed research, loved talking to people and learning about all the things that happened to them. In fact, sometimes I have had to tone down the plot twists because they were so unbelievable that no one would accept them as fact.

"My husband's job wound up getting transferred to Washington D.C. and that's about as far away from Hollywood as you can get. So I hooked up with Carolyn Turner and started a screenwriters group for the local Women in Film chapter. This was a great move in terms of networking and I told everyone I met that I did true stories, so it worked both ways. People wound up coming to me looking for true stories and they also sent people to me if they had a story to tell. It was a great experience for me because I learned a lot about what people wanted to hear when it came to having their story told. I also learned how to effectively interview people, how to get their stories out of them, and how to tell them in a way that would sell.

"When you are a new writer, you want to write so many different things but the problem is that you can't be good at everything. I've focused on true stories, but now I am starting to refocus on doing thrillers, many of which are based on true crimes. I think that the more you work in a genre the better you get at it and you have to have a specialty to make it in this industry. The competition is incredible and I'm always amazed at how many scripts are floating around out there. Despite the volume, there's a tremendous amount of bad scripts out there because people always focus on the same stuff—the Mafia, drugs, battered women—and you can't sell them anymore, even if they are true stories. Unless there is a completely new twist that hasn't been seen before, any true story is a tough sell, no matter how weird or unbelievable it is. But true thrillers and crime stories almost always sell because it's unusual to start with and the behavior is often fascinating and has a twist in it. I usually look for original stories, but I have adapted books as well. Since I have a reputation for doing this, people call me from all over— Alaska, Kansas, Missouri, everywhere—with their experiences. I also like to look in papers in the Midwest for material, but never look in the Los Angeles papers anymore because of the competition. If it appears in an L.A. paper, it's gone before the ink is dry.

"Still, selling anything in Hollywood is tough. It's a small community and there are only so many movies made each year. But true stories offer an advantage because people are more likely to talk to you if you have the rights to someone's life story. Production companies are worried about lawsuits and the fact that you have the rights eliminates a lot of problems for them right from the start. That's why they often look at adapting books. There's a big market for that, especially if the book has sold well. In Hollywood, people like to have books because they can hold it in their hand and it shows that someone else took a risk on it. Since the industry is risk-averse, it makes it easier for someone to sell it to the network or their own boss in a production company because someone else thought enough of the idea to publish it and it's easier to option the story from the author than it is from three or four different people who were involved in the story. At any given moment, I have twenty-five different stories going under an option agreement. I typically option the life story and then don't pay the person until I sell it to a production company. If you did it any other way, you'd go broke in a hurry.

"If you're a writer out here, you need an agent. Finding an agent is always tough. I've had three and I can tell you that there's no one way to get one that has always worked. The basic thing is that you have to get someone interested in your work. At one point in my career, I decided that I didn't need an agent and was on my own, but that's not the way to go. As a writer, you really do need an agent because without one you spend more time trying to get your foot in the door than you do writing and that's what you need to be doing—writing."

Steve White

Steve White Productions

White went out on his own after nearly a decade as an executive in network television. Originally an agent who represented writers specializing in television movies, he joined ABC in 1980 before moving over to NBC to work for Grant Tinker and running that network's movie and miniseries divisions for several years. He formed his own production company in the early 1990s and was recently joined by his wife, who had been running the Lifetime Channel's movie operations. Many of White's recent movies have been based on true crime incidents. "There's an endless fascination on the part of both the producers and the viewers when it comes to these kinds of movies. People are captivated with the prospect of learning how ordinary people can commit these horrible crimes."

* * * * *

"True stories, especially ones having to do with crimes, have always been the staple of the television movie genre. In part, it's what the audience expects us to do, to tell dramatic true stories about ordinary people and some of those will inevitably involve people who were murdered. Sometimes people will watch something that they would not want to happen to them, but they do it because it offers them a safe way of exploring that emotion. Yet I've noticed that as we've had a period of sustained prosperity, people have become less interested in violent, aberrant behavior and are more interested in stories that reflect a quality of life theme. Just look at *The English Patient* or the other top-rated films today. They're all Sunday night hallmarks, warm, uplifting stories about life, and I think they reflect a direct link to the current economic tides. People aren't as frustrated as they were a few years ago and that has an impact on the type of entertainment they want to see. A lot of things drive the cycles this business goes through, and economics is certainly one of them.

"In my experience, the best true-life stories always seem to come out of Texas and Florida, especially violent murder stories. We read the out-of-town papers from both these states and we get a lot of stories from them, plus from books about cases and other sources. These vary, but can include such things as the national media—papers, magazines, advance galleys of books, blurbs in *Publishers Weekly*, those sorts of things. But two things are changing when it comes to developing a true story. The first is the growing amount of prime time available to news coverage because of the success of the newsmagazine format. Right now I think there's at least ten hours of that programming a week and they often get the jump over anyone who can write a book. In a lot of cases, the story's already been told by the time a writer gets to the scene. We used to look for books as a source, but now it's more direct from the media itself. So when we find something, it's either the story that no one saw because it didn't hit the media or it was complicated and took more research than they were willing to put into a ten-minute story. There can also be a story that wasn't apparent in the media and those are the stories that we pick up from books. Then there's the whole field of fiction crime writing. That's growing because so many writers are getting scooped out by the media and it is where a lot of books get bought these days, especially if there's a good character or plot. A lot of times, writers will take a true story or elements of true stories and then fictionalize them instead of spending years researching a true story that's been overpublicized in the press. They'll have good characters that are on 'our' side—the judges, prosecutors, reporters, or detectives—and then work them into a story. John Grisham does that a lot.

"The biggest challenge in doing these kind of productions is finding material that is new or different or truly illuminates the human condition as opposed to material that just recapitulates the facts or is overly familiar. I always look for classical tragic themes, universal themes that we can all relate to, that catches us up in a person's story. But the classic problem in adapting these stories is when the real event isn't dramatic enough, when things don't happen in the right order or there are motivations that you need to explain because the behaviors that would do it aren't present. That's why we have to use writers who are experts at this kind of work. There's a whole group of very talented writers who do nothing but write television movies. They adapt from a novel or a nonfiction book or from research materials and write directly from that. We'll often send out to meet the real people and get transcripts from trials and we'll do the same research that a nonfiction writer would do to write a book. But we just put it in a format that works to keep an audience tuned in and away from changing the channel."

Index

From Book Idea to Bestseller

What You Absolutely, Positively Must Know to Make Your Book a Success

Michael Snell, Kim Baker, Sunny Baker

ISBN 0-7615-0630-6 / paperback / 432 pages
U.S. $18.00 / Can. $24.95

These nonfiction specialists know what they're talking about. Michael Snell is a literary agent credited in over 300 books and the author or co-author of 34 books. Kim and Sunny Baker have authored 23 books, including several on desktop publishing. They understand what today's authors need to know: It takes more than good writing to get published, and it takes more than publication to get to the top of the bestseller lists. Learn how to work with publishers to get your book accepted and make it sell. Here's how it's done—every step of the way!

The WRITER'S GUIDE Series

Prima's WRITER'S GUIDE books name names and give addresses, phone and fax numbers, and other essential information to put you in touch with the people who can put your work in print!

Writer's Guide to Book Editors, Publishers, and Literary Agents, 1998–1999

This top seller includes inside information about how agents agree to represent writers, how publishers acquire books, and how editors help shape them. It also has a directory of hundreds of book publishers.

ISBN 0-7615-1012-5
paperback / 984 pages
U.S. $25.00 / Can. $33.95

Writer's Guide to Software Developers, Electronic Publishers, and Agents, 1997–1998

Electronic publishing is taking off, and more and more savvy writers are riding the new medium to success. Find out who the electronic publishers are and what they're looking for. You'll also get a detailed list of agents who specialize in electronic projects.

ISBN 0-7615-0062-6
paperback / 352 pages
U.S. $23.00 / Can. $29.95

Writer's Guide to Hollywood Producers, Directors, and Screenwriter's Agents

Aspiring screenwriters and established pros turn to this book for the inside information they need to break into Hollywood and stay on top once they get there. Includes an extensive directory, interviews, and tips on formatting and structure.

ISBN 0-7615-0399-4
paperback / 416 pages
U.S. $23.00 / Can. $29.95

Writer's Guide to Magazine Editors and Publishers, 1997–1998

You'll find every major periodical represented in here, as well as many niche and trade publications. Each is described in detail with contacts, submission requirements, and individual pay rates. Several magazine editors contributed their own practical insights in informative essays.

ISBN 0-7615-0409-5
paperback / 416 pages
U.S. $23.00 / Can. $29.95

Visit us online at www.primapublishing.com

To Order Books

Please send me the following items:

Quantity	Title	Unit Price	Total
_____	Writer's Guide to Book Editors	$ __25.00__	$ _____
_____	Writer's Guide to Software Developers	$ __23.00__	$ _____
_____	Writer's Guide to Hollywood Producers	$ __23.00__	$ _____
_____	Writer's Guide to Magazine Editors	$ __23.00__	$ _____
_____	_____	$ _____	$ _____

*Shipping and Handling depend on Subtotal.

Subtotal	Shipping/Handling
$0.00–$14.99	$3.00
$15.00–$29.99	$4.00
$30.00–$49.99	$6.00
$50.00–$99.99	$10.00
$100.00–$199.99	$13.50
$200.00+	Call for Quote

Foreign and all Priority Request orders:
Call Order Entry department
for price quote at 916-632-4400

This chart represents the total retail price of books only (before applicable discounts are taken).

Subtotal $ _____

Deduct 10% when ordering 3-5 books $ _____

7.25% Sales Tax (CA only) $ _____

8.25% Sales Tax (TN only) $ _____

5.0% Sales Tax (MD and IN only) $ _____

7.0% G.S.T. Tax (Canada only) $ _____

Shipping and Handling* $ _____

Total Order $ _____

By Telephone: With MC or Visa, call 800-632-8676 or 916-632-4400.
Mon–Fri, 8:30-4:30.

WWW: http://www.primapublishing.com

By Internet E-mail: sales@primapub.com

By Mail: Just fill out the information below and send with your remittance to:

Prima Publishing
P.O. Box 1260BK
Rocklin, CA 95677

My name is _____

I live at _____

City _____ State _____ ZIP _____

MC/Visa#_____ Exp. _____

Check/money order enclosed for $_____ Payable to Prima Publishing

Daytime telephone _____

Signature _____